The

Enki

Chronicles

Ushering in a New Age

A novel by

T Raphael Evans

You are in physical existence to learn and understand that your energy, translated into feelings, thoughts and emotions causes all experiences. There are no exceptions - Seth

Consider if you will, that the universe is infinite. This has yet to be proven or disproven, but we can assure you that there is no end to yourselves, your understanding, what you call your journey of seeking, or your perception of the creation – Ra

And it came to pass, when men began to multiply on the face of the Earth and daughters were born unto them, that the sons of God saw the daughters of men that they were fair, and they took them wives of all which they chose. There were giants upon the Earth in those days and also thereafter too, When the sons of God came in unto the daughters of men and they bare children to them— the same Mighty Men of old, Men of Renown – Genesis Chapter 6, King James version

The search for answers started with linguistic questions. The Hebrew text does not speak of "Men" who began to multiply, but of Ha'Adam—"The Adam," a generic term, a human species. It does not speak of the sons of "God," but uses the term Bnei Ha-Elohim— the sons (in the plural) of The Elohim, a plural term taken to mean "gods" but literally meaning "The Lofty Ones." The "Daughters of The Adam" were not "fair," but Tovoth—good, compatible . . . And unavoidably we find ourselves confronting issues of origins. How did Mankind happen to be on this planet, and whose genetic code do we carry? - Zecharia Sitchin

Prologue

Have you ever wondered what it would be like to meet a real, modern- day prophet? What if Elijah or Isaiah came back in blue jeans and a tee-shirt? Would we recognize them or better yet would we believe what they had to say? What would we need from such a person to believe they were truly a messenger sent by the Almighty?

If such a person were spat out on Bondi Beach by a whale shark would everyone in Australia be in awe and listen intently to what this fellow might say? The news of this event might spread around the world instantaneously on Twitter or Facebook and a new age would usher in. Or ten thousand investigative reporters would descend upon the poor fellow and determine that he was an imposter.

If this person were to command fire from heaven and consume a Buddhist temple would this be proof of a divine mission or just piss-off a lot of monks.

It's hard to believe that in the 21st century with instant worldwide communication that the depiction of a real event whether on TV or some other media outlet could amaze all of us in the same way.

If people in North America are expecting Jesus Christ to return (Asia and the Middle East do not expect such a thing and Europe doesn't care) what would that look like? Hopefully not anything like what happened to the Incas who were expecting Quetzalcoatl's return but instead had their heads handed to them by Cortes.

If there were a great conflagration in the sky and out of it came a mysterious figure one might imagine the Muslims praying, 'Please God, let it be Mohammed', while the Christians would be praying,

'Please God, let it be Jesus', while the Jews might be praying,
'Please God, let it be Elijah'.

But if someone sat down beside you at an outdoor cantina and told
you, in a laid back conversational manner that he was a Sumerian
god returning to Earth to warn of a coming worldwide upheaval.
Would you laugh and move to another table. Would you sit politely
and listen, then at the first sign of a break in the conversation, run.

If you saw him again and he continued with his story and it actually
started to make sense, then would you believe it? What kind of sign
would you ask of him or what miraculous event would convince you
that he was indeed a god?

If he showed you things that you didn't think possible, would you
believe him or doubt your own sanity. Would you share this
experience with your family and friends or keep it to yourself for
fear of being institutionalized?

Do you think this could happen?

Jim was a fellow who had grown up in a normal well rounded
Catholic family in the Midwest. His childhood years were
enlightened by the teachings of the Catholic Church but as he grew
into his teenage years the whole idea of grace, sacrifice and
atonement just didn't work for him anymore. Jim realized that
what he saw in the real world did not match his Christian belief in
how the world was supposed to work. So without a thought beyond
that which is normal for a young man with his sights set on beer,
football and adventure, he discarded his Christian beliefs.

As things happen Jim eventually got married had kids and worked a
normal job. Everything was going well, that is, until an evangelical
preacher came into his life. Jim didn't think too much about God or

doctrine and all that religious stuff but the preacher convinced him to start thinking about it which was enough to bring him back into the waiting arms of the church.

But after many years of drifting through patterns of belief and disbelief, Jim found himself in a spot where the meaning of life became muddled again. He started to question everything he believed. This was the start of Jim's journey of self-discovery.

Then his life took an interesting twist when he encountered a charismatic, enigmatic person that caused him to look deep inside himself and challenge everything that he thought was normal. What Jim didn't realize however was that his new friend was preparing him for the ultimate experience of his life.

Introduction

My story started as a journey into beliefs. Beliefs that started with the reflection of my own life and how religion and philosophy affected me. They seemed to define how I was supposed to view the world and myself.

The success that I saw, as judged in the newspaper or by the abundance of TV shows sought to define who I was, or better yet, who I wanted to be.

I watched with glee, Hollywood's impression of success in a stunningly diverse portrayal of peoples' lives. I sat in front of my TV allowing Hollywood to define for me what constituted success. If I flipped to CNN Financial, they would define what success meant from a different viewpoint.

Arnold was hugely successful in both the roles he played in movies and his real life which was quite an accomplishment for a poor Austrian boy with gifted genetics and a positive attitude towards life. He was a role model to the many young men who looked up to him. He was able to achieve seemingly whatever he set his sights on except when it came down to his marriage. Was this success? Hard to ascertain since the definition of success has been so skewed. After all, Arnold is still rich and famous and Tiger still gets cheered every time he hits a straight drive. So it might seem that the sanctity of marriage does not factor into the equation for success.

Another character that was fabulously successful and resonated with practically everyone was the Dude. A man of his time, somewhat lazy and a bit of an alcoholic but hugely successful as the little Lebowski. A man standing up for his rights and not allowing his rug to be urinated on. A symbol for all of us to stand up for.

There are millionaires and billionaires that suggest money has a part to play in our view of success. Should we seek out the billions that Bill Gates, Warren Buffett or Mark Zuckerberg has achieved to define ourselves as successful? Even if we tone it down a notch or two and consider that millions are more achievable, is that something to strive for?

I grew up in a well rounded middle income Catholic family. I had two brothers and two sisters and we went to church every Sunday. On those same Sundays my older brother was apt to have an unusual amount of spare change on his person and wine on his breath. He was an altar boy and the church was always a little light on collection when he was on duty. My brother was also smart enough to know that the confessional was an institution introduced by the papacy in medieval times to keep track of things going on around the village and had nothing to do with God. So, with clear conscience, he not only learned to steal and drink within the confines of the Catholic Church, but also became a prolific liar as well.

He would go to confession and lie about things that he had done then lie about things he hadn't done just to even it out.

On the other hand, I took confession seriously. As a young devout fellow I would head to church on a Friday night to have my confession heard while the other guys were out with their girlfriends at the A&W having root beers. I would tell the good Reverend about the dark and dubious things that I had not only done but also thought of doing. Somewhere along the line I was taught that thoughts about doing things were every bit as heinous to God as the actual doing of those things.

Afterwards the Rev would have a few words of encouragement and then give me penance to the tune of 11 or 12 'Hail Marys' and 15 or 20 'Our Fathers'. The prayers were related to the sin so as to nullify or neutralize the ugliness in God's eyes. I think. Seemingly, the 'Our Fathers' were less valuable than the 'Hail Marys' since you had to say more of them. I likened this to the Canadian dollar versus the American dollar.

It occurred to me many years later that if I toned down the things I was telling the Reverend, there would be fewer "Hail Marys" and "Our Fathers" and I could get out faster. It never occurred to me, like it had with my brother, that if I didn't say any of the prayers or lied about what I had done, the good Lord wouldn't mind because he was busy. Everybody is busy and he's busy too.

But I stopped going to church when I was about 16 years old when one fateful Sunday morning my mom announced, very solemnly that I was old enough to make my own decision whether to attend church or not. I remember answering in an equally solemn manner that I would not attend, at least for now, and that I would reconsider at a later date. That was my outward reply but inwardly it was a giant Yaaaahooooo as there would now be time to recover from hangovers. No more pious lectures from the pulpit and no more confession – thank god. My brother kept going because his loss in revenue would have been substantial.

About 10 years later after marrying a wonderful woman and moving to a new city, I found myself sitting across from the good reverend of a local Presbyterian Church discussing the attributes of Christianity from the protestant point of view.

Since the blessed fellow was a hopelessly dedicated evangelical, well educated in apologetics and most of all devout, he encouraged me to re-commit myself to the church. I used to wonder what evangelical meant but after my encounter with the good vicar it was clear that the word meant teaching all the interesting and good things about Jesus to people who didn't necessarily want to know or didn't really care.

One of my great realizations however, after being in the Presbyterian church for a few years was that it was far easier to be Catholic than Presbyterian. As a Catholic you could do a lot of really stupid shit all week long then spend maybe an hour or two at the confessional. You would say your 'Hail Marys' and then you're right with the Lord. He had forgiven you and the week started anew with a rejuvenated soul.

As a Presbyterian however there was pressure to be good in the eyes of God all the time. You must try to be like Jesus even though no one can be like him 'cause he's too good. But still you must try. There was no confessional so you had to be careful that the sins didn't pile up too high.

As a result, I found myself walking around with a smile on my face and always trying to be nice to everyone. This was not my basic nature. My basic nature was that of a douche bag. I didn't like being nice, in fact, I liked to make fun of people, argue about stuff, drink and do all sorts of stupid things.

As a Catholic I could be myself all week long then on Friday night, confession followed by a few 'Our Fathers' had me back to square one with the Lord. But as a Presbyterian, there was no such thing so I felt destined for hell.

I guess that's why the mafia and the drug lords are all Catholic.

It seemed Presbyterianism was my lot in life and after several years of study and devotion my dedication did not go unnoticed and behold, I was asked to be an elder. Not knowing exactly what an elder was (I wasn't that old at the time) or what was needed to do an elder's job (something about being extra nice to people, I think), as fate would have it, I changed jobs and moved to another town.

 A funny thing happened however, as I got further away from the influence of that one saintly man, I began to sense that something was amiss in the whole scheme of things. Something like common sense and logic. I say this in the nicest possible way but when I studied the Old Testament and tried to relate it to the New Testament, things got real fuzzy and nonsensical. It was then I realized that I was doing the only thing that allows a sane, otherwise intelligent man or woman to believe in the Holy Bible and all of its stories and claims without tossing it out as a poor, abstract, divisive compilation of myths. It's called rationalization.

When something awful happens in the world, like a wild fire roasting 257 innocent people to death, you have to wonder who's in charge. Then we hear in the news every day about murders, mass murders and senseless killings to go along with the usual greed and financial skulduggery. Either I was missing something or I was not interpreting correctly how things are supposed to work.

I didn't find answers in the Bible. But at the same time I was terrified at the thought of leaving the companionship and comfort of the church.

I found it difficult to rationalize a loving God in control of the mayhem that seemed to occur day to day. Many people, seemingly reasonable people, and maybe even smart people, believe every word of the bible to be true. What is fundamental to Christianity is that God is in control and loves us all. How could this be? I faithfully believed it, up to a point and then it got blurry.

Sept. 11, 2001 arrived and the world stood in horror at the senseless loss of life. I stood dumbfounded as I watched footage on TV of planes crashing into the World Trade Centre. I continued to be dumbfounded as the conspiracy theories hit the internet soon thereafter with every conceivable situation explored. The newspaper stories and documentaries were there for our examination telling tales of heroism and luck. Lucky for those that phoned in sick that day and heroic for those that sacrificed their lives to save others. In fact there were so many varied and gripping stories come out of this tragedy that it truly was the event of the decade.

Spin the will of God into the yarn and it became impossible to understand the events as they unfolded. Some survived and some didn't so I wondered if the Christian and Jewish God Yahweh, protected some but not all. Were the ones that survived special to the almighty while those that died, sinners and abhorrent in his sight?

Were atheists among the majority killed, how about Muslims or Hindu's? Maybe most of the people killed were Christians so perhaps it shouldn't surprise anyone that Jehovah singled out his own people for destruction as he had done on many previous occasions. The Babylonians had been a tool of destruction as were the Assyrians so it didn't seem like a stretch for me to believe this scenario.

I contemplated that God, as revealed in the Old Testament and New Testament could not possibly have been involved in Sept. 11. How could he? Frankly there have been atrocities perpetrated against humankind for many millennia and this was just another in a string of hopelessly senseless mass murders brought about by fanatics. But this was different. There were Jews, Muslim, Christians, Hindus and Atheists killed in the attack. How could this be the work of a single God? There either had to be many gods at work or none.

As much as I tried to rationalize how a god, any god could have participated in the enactment of the events of Sept 11, I was perplexed and couldn't get past the irony of a supposedly loving god. Equally perplexing was a god that stood down.

Maybe the lord god Jehovah really was a war god invented by a tribe of people 3000 years ago who were continuously surrounded by enemies. At that time everyone needed a war god and this one belonged to an incredibly robust and enduring people. I just couldn't see how an ancient war god could still be relevant.

Who can know the mind of God or random chance were just not good explanations for what happened in New York. So after many sessions of personalized internal thought I concluded that it was possible there was no Jehovah, no Allah, no Buddha and no Krishna. It was also possible that they were all actively involved in the affairs of man and sat at the same table. Maybe even Zeus, Marduk and Isis sat there as well.

I had the sense that perhaps there was a viable alternative to religious thought. I was a little unsure if I was wrong and there was a big guy in the sky named Yahweh. Doomed to everlasting eternal hellfire, seething in agony with my hair aflame was a distinct possibility. I had to hold that up against the possibility that heaven and hell were merely constructs of the church. After all, there was no proof.

It did not become an obsession nor do I think it ever became a passion, but over time, and with the help of a few good books to nurture the thought process along, a notion began to formulate in my head. A realization that perhaps there might just be something else. It might be that we are starting to learn all over again something that perhaps we have forgotten for many centuries about who we are and what we are doing here.

That's when I realized that there were probably a lot of people like me. People who were inbetween religion and reality and didn't know which way to turn. I started to call myself an inbetween man since I was somewhere inbetween Christianity, Atheism and whatever else was out there. I thought that Paganism was kinda cool too.

The 'whatever else' was a dangerous place as this was the domain of the crackpot. This was where the Jim Jones' of the world lurked and one had to be careful.

Religion had always been a part of my life and there were certainly some good things about it. Christians celebrated Christmas and Easter while Mormons had a total focus on family. Jehovah Witness didn't allow Santa Claus into their house but had a wonderful sense of destiny and who can forget the Pentecostals. I would love to listen to someone speak in tongues and pass snakes around. At the Presbyterian Church all we did was sing songs.

For me, religion did not give the answers, but there was something in the air and I could feel it, almost taste it. There was a feeling that something special was on the horizon and I realized that there are more people on the face of the earth today than at any time in the history of the world. Was that special? What if we are all here for the same reason, to witness something spectacular and unique?

What that was, I had no idea but then something very curious
happened.......I met Enki.

Chapter 1: My First Encounter

My personal journey was made difficult in a way that I could never have imagined as it started out on such a positive note. I was a regular guy, raising what seemed like a perfect family with a wife and four well rounded kids. At least they weren't drug addicts (that I knew of) so when an opportunity came along, a chance to work abroad, it was a no-brainer.

I was horribly bored at my previous job which was a serious character flaw I will freely admit and this was a chance to revitalize myself. The job took me to a tropical climate where there were brightly coloured birds, beaches, sun and more importantly, cheap beer. Err, I mean a challenging job that had me back on a learning curve. The prospects were exciting and invigorating, then a few years later, as abruptly as the job came into being, it ended.

This caused me to embark on a rather disjointed and somewhat precarious journey in search of new work and new challenges but as it would turn out, the journey was in search of myself more than anything.

Then an interesting twist came along as I had an opportunity to work on a project in Vietnam to develop a manufacturing facility. Vietnam is an interesting place where almost anything goes and the people are dedicated to making a better life for themselves after years of war and abject poverty.

I worked away for about 2 years but this project too had come to an end. I found myself in a situation with several days to kill before going home. So I started a routine of riding my motorcycle into downtown Hanoi to sit at a little outdoor pub on the lake in the heart of the downtown tourist area which was aptly named the French Quarter. It was abundant with taxis, street vendors, shops and stores. A beautiful spot it was and my little pub served cheap cold beer so my afternoons were an exercise in contemplation, revelation and libation.

One interesting aspect of drinking a cold drink in a hot, humid tropical climate is that if you are not quick enough and I mean fast on the guzzle, the beer becomes tepid and ice cubes are required. The act of putting ice in beer is a travesty and no less than a mortal sin that would quickly have you on that wide road to hell in my way of thinking. However, since it was after 1:00PM (and especially hot), I was avoiding ice by putting them (the beers I mean) away before they got cold, in other words, at a torrid pace.

 It was then that a man who seemed of European descent stopped by my table and asked if he could sit for a bit since I had a nice table off to the side with an umbrella that offered shade from the sun but not from the ever present humidity. Had the man been Vietnamese, I would have sent him quickly on his way as Vietnamese always stopped by to chat and try to sell something.

This fellow was quite different with dark hair, intense blue eyes, dark olive skin and tall slim features perhaps indicating Italian lineage. Most striking was his height which was well over 6.5 feet but not quite 7. As he began talking I tried to pick up the accent which was thick and noticeable but completely unrecognizable. With such auspicious beginnings I thought that at least a quick conversation was worth the effort since I had nothing else to do and it didn't appear as if he wanted to sell me anything.

"May I sit," he asked politely.

"You may," I returned, "Can I offer to buy you a sample of what's on tap today."

"Sure," replied my new friend in a somewhat strange and unqualified accent.

The waitress had come and gone with the order of still yet another beer for me and a fresh one for my new friend.

Since my curiosity had gotten the better of me, the first thing that came out of my mouth was what had stoked my interest from the beginning, "That's quite the accent you have my friend, where are you from, may I ask?"

"Well," he replied, "I am a long way from home and for all intents and purposes, let's just say I am from Mesopotamia."

"Mesopotamia?" I replied, "Can't say I have heard that one before since most folk I've met are usually from countries that are currently in existence. Now correct me if I am wrong but wasn't Mesopotamia an area existing in ancient times in what is now southern Iraq?"

"Yes, well done, you've got it," replied my new friend, "and furthermore it is an area rich in history and lore. An area that has received some attention but not enough to warrant the relative importance that is it's due."

"But Mesopotamia and its culture and people haven't been in existence for 3000 years, so how can you be from a place that exists as layers of rubble in the deserts of Iraq?" I said in a somewhat bewildered and half inebriated state.

The little Vietnamese waitress returned and plunked down 2 large frosty pints just as the day had grown decidedly hotter and the humidity took a turn for the worse. In Hanoi the humidity is either bad or really bad and it settles like an anvil, some days, thick and heavy, not too unlike being inside a pressure cooker.

"To the gods," I said as was customary for me to say lifting the frosty mug to my parched lips. I had always pictured myself in a previous life in ancient Rome sitting around a big table in a toga with my fellow Romans offering libation to the gods.

A curious look came over my new friend's face, one that was of surprise and delight, 'To the gods'," he said. "Now what is your name?"

"Jim," I replied, "And yours?"

"Enki," was his reply.

"Enki?" I must have sounded a bit confused, "Enki is not that usual a name and I am not one to judge this or that but I have only heard that name one other time and that was in ancient Sumeria. Enki was a major deity who ruled essentially all of mankind along with his brother Enlil. Enki was the god of water and the god of wisdom. Are you named after Enki the Sumerian god?"

"No," was his reply, "I am not named after Enki, I am Enki. The same that you describe."

I looked at him expecting his sparkling eyes would begin to squint, bright white teeth would show and a huge guffaw would erupt sending us both into fits of laughter followed by glugs of beer. It didn't happen.

What the hell, I thought to myself, I am in the presence of a god, or perhaps a lunatic. I wondered if he was selling contraband cigars after all. I was looking for a good box of Cohibas.

"OKaaaay," I said. "But you don't look like a god."

"What does a god look like? He replied. "Am I supposed to be 8 feet tall and wear white robes?"

"Good point," I said. "But you are just about 7 feet by my estimation. How am I supposed to believe that you are who you say you are? Please forgive my candour, but *if* I was sitting with a god would you not be able to show me something that would be incredulous, other than that outrageous accent. Something that no one else, no ordinary person could do. Maybe guzzle that beer in less than 2 seconds."

"Well, look at it this way," my new friend said. "When we first arrived on what you now call Earth, we called it Tiamet, we were for all intents and purposes the first human-like creatures to set foot on this planet. There was a small group of partial humans that lived in caves but truly we were just normal guys looking for a bit of yellow metal. Meanwhile the cavemen as you call them were just trying to keep from being eaten by animals.

So when these first humanoids saw us and realized that we didn't have four legs, fangs and claws and weren't going to eat them, they kind of liked us.

Since we were much taller and our clothing was more fashionable than animal skins, the caveman came to look upon us favourably. They might have even thought we were superior to them, which of course, we were.

But nobody asked us to walk on water or shoot lightning bolts out of our fingertips to prove our superiority as there was no frame of reference at that time to what a god was or what a god could or couldn't do.

They were unable to distinguish an imposter from a true god. They could only see that we were different. The animals that were around at that time couldn't have cared less about who or what we were. Since we were flesh and blood, the predators around at that time were just as happy to eat us as they were the caveman. The only difference was that we had what you would refer to as laser guns instead of spears."

My third beer must have evaporated because I honestly did not remember drinking it. As I contemplated the disappearance of my beer it occurred to me that surly one of us was a crackpot and I wasn't sure if it was my new friend for pretending to be a Sumerian god or me for almost believing him.

He seemed to sense what I was thinking and said, "Back in the beginning it was not our wish to portray ourselves as gods. We had come for gold as you call it. Our intention was to extract as much as we could then get back to our home planet.

However, sitting with you here today is different. Telling you who I am is strictly between you and me, not for anyone else. I am telling you that I am a Sumerian god because I am. But I would not portray myself as such to everyone at this time.

I have no need to show anyone on this planet that I have special attributes or powers as you say. I will show *you* certain things that you need to see and then you can decide if I am who I say I am. You will need to have a great capacity for comprehension and an open mind like never before."

After Enki had finished talking he took a sip of his beer and gazed across the lake as if deep in thought.

I wasn't sure now if Enki was saying that he was or wasn't a Sumerian god. It sounded like if it suited his desires he could be a god but mostly just wanted to be a regular guy.

That seemed like a fair cop since walking around saying stuff like "behold" or "verily, verily", might seem lame and not get the results he was looking for. But what was he looking for?

It did seem a little weird that if he was a god that had returned to save mankind or whatever, why he only wanted to reveal himself to me?

But he would have to prove himself a god to convince me. He would have to do something pretty special that our technologically advanced society could not reproduce. We have electric pepper grinders for god's sake, how could he possibly outdo that?

But as I was contemplating my sanity (he was quite sure of his) I remembered some of the details I had read in the voluminous works of Zecharia Sitchen.

Sitchen was author of the Earth Chronicles, an extensive and exhaustive work pertaining to ancient Sumeria. He was one of a handful of scholars who was able to translate the ancient cuneiform language of Sumeria into modern day English. The archaeological digs performed in southern Iraq unearthed what is currently believed to be the remains of ancient cities of Sumeria. Over 14,000 clay tablets, cylinders and fragments were found amongst the ruins describing in uncanny detail its society, laws, morality and gods. Enki and his brother Enlil were right at the top of the pantheon of gods described.

Since I had read some of Sitchen's work, I thought it might be a way to quickly smoke out my friend's predisposition as a self-proclaimed deity. At the very least, if he knows as much about Sumeria as current information would dictate, then we can at least talk intelligently about that instead of this silly god nonsense.

"Enki," I began, "May I ask a few questions about your past experiences as a god in ancient Sumeria?"

"I expect nothing less," he replied in his funny clipped accent. He kind of sounded like Brad Pitt in Inglorious Bastards trying to combine an Italian accent with a southern drawl.

"Well, let's start at the beginning. When you first landed on Earth, what did you see, who was here, what did it look like and why did you come? I know you told me about the gold but could you kindly expand."

"Good place to start. We came in search of gold as I said. Our scientists determined that we needed it to preserve our atmosphere back on our home planet Nibiru. A scout discovered the presence of gold on Tiamet and I volunteered to make the long dangerous trip to investigate. And behold, I found vast quantities of gold in your oceans that even today still exists but unobtainable due to its dilution. I then later discovered vast reserves of gold in what you now called South Africa. We named the area Abzu.

When we landed on the planet's surface there were no humanoids, at least what we could determine by our initial scans. I started by establishing a colony which I named Eridu. My brother Enlil came later and by drawing lots we established that he would be lord of Earth and I lord of the seas. I was also in charge of extracting the gold.

As gold production dramatically increased, a second wave of men from Nibiru arrived to work in the mines. This caused much dissension amongst those whose lot was to work underground and so they began to grumble. About the same time as my sister Ninmah arrived from Nibiru I had discovered a primitive tribe of what you would call cavemen in the area of the mines which had escaped notice on our first scan.

The grumbling of fellow Annunaki (what we called ourselves), the arrival of Ninmah and the discovery of a race of indigenous earthlings provided me with an opportunity to fix our problem. Since Ninmah and I were trained in genetics, it was my idea to splice our own Annunaki chromosomes into that of the resident caveman to produce a worker race to replace our fellow countrymen in the mines. After much trial and error, Ninmah and I were successful and we named our new creation the Adamu.

What neither I nor Ninmah realized at the time was that we had significantly increased the evolutionary progress of this early species of mankind. Not only that but we had unwittingly created the ideal chemical complex for mind/spirit entities to inhabit. Therefore we unknowingly advanced Earth's evolutionary process by millions of years and that is why today your evolutionary scientists cannot find the missing link between Neanderthal/Cro-Magnon man and Homo sapien. It is because in geological time, it literally happened over night. There is no link."

"Can we have a couple more beers," I politely asked the Vietnamese waitress who seemed quite bored by this time. In Vietnam the servers rarely serve. It's like they actually do not want to sell you more cold beer. I was never able to understand if it was a cultural thing or if every server in the country was completely bored to death.

After briefly contemplating the service industry in Vietnam my attention came back to Enki's story. I was astounded. Everything he said up to this point was crazy, wild and you would have to be a madman to accept this supposition. Maybe he knew a little of Sitchen's work as I did, but there was something about him that I couldn't put a finger on.

"You lost me on the part about mind/spirit complex," I went on to say after receiving acknowledgement that the beer was on its way.

Enki continued, "What most humans do not realize, even today with your sophisticated instruments and so-called higher learning, is that each and every one of you are made up of 3 parts. Without all three, you cannot function as normal."

"That would explain a few people I know," I interrupted.

"Yes, well let's just say that mind/body/spirit is the secret formula for evolution. When I first encountered the primitive man on earth which you call Neanderthal, he was basically a second density beast whose primary concern was survival. My race the Annunaki were 3rd density beings at the time but our understanding of what that meant was rudimentary. There was no clarity amongst the majority of our people. Not too unlike what you and most other humans are experiencing now.

When Ninmah and I spliced our chromosomes into the cave-man, we effectively allowed the progress of this species to accelerate to 3rd density or what you would call an awareness of self, which to begin with, allows the being to contemplate its existence beyond mere survival.

It is interesting for me now to see how you have progressed and especially interesting to contemplate what may have happened had we not interfered with your normal evolutionary progress. The best I can ascertain would be something akin to your Hollywood movie called "Planet of the Apes". This depicts an evolutionary probability that apes may have progressed quicker than the cave-man and may have possibly created a situation in which the apes become lords over man, that is, had we not found gold."

"Am I to understand then, that you are saying, the Lord God Jehovah in Old Testament did not create man _ you did," I said incredulously.

 "That's right."

"So where did the cave-man come from before you and your sister messed around with his DNA? The primordial soup, a billion years earlier, perhaps?"

 "No. Life originates in two different manners. First, life exists as a seed with all the genetic material necessary to grow an infinitely diverse set of life forms given the proper nutrients and conditions. Just like a mighty oak grows out of a small pod. These seeds are spread out across the universe and to understand how this happens or where the seeds come from I need to explain many other things first. So we will come back to this later.

The second way is when conscious energy manifests itself as flesh and blood creatures of its own choosing in order to experience a new existence. Entities existing as energy gestalts try different forms that match the environment and then choose the right one that best suit their needs. Other energy forms see the success and copy it.

The original humanoid, the caveman, may have been seeded from somewhere else in the galaxy which I am not privy to but let me say that everything in the universe is alive and once you realize this, it is not a stretch to comprehend the seed of man coming from outside the planet's atmosphere. Then other entities came later that were manifestations of energy gestalts."

"I'll admit," I said, "there is a mindset amongst our intellectuals that suggests we are the only ones in the universe and we originated from the basic elements that exist on the planet."

"That is absurd since anyone can see that it takes intelligent energy to form the building blocks of life from no matter where it comes. However, let me back up a bit and explain in a little more detail some of the things you have obviously read regarding creation.

First you must realize that the clay tablets we purposely left behind in our ancient cities of long ago, gave what you would call a mythical description of our activities intermixed with precise information on all matters of government, law, morality, history and society.

The clay tablets gave descriptions of the gods and their activities in a language format that was familiar to us at the time and therefore may not be completely understood by future civilizations. These clay tablets predate the earliest writings in your bible and in my estimation; Zecharia Sitchen did a good job of translating the tablets into modern day language.

So the various authors of the bible borrowed information from an already established history of things as determined by what we had previously written. Your modern historians and scientists will agree with this statement. So with that in mind, let me tell you about a man named Abram who lived in Ur which was a city in Sumeria.

This will help you understand how many separate civilizations and religions were really just one.

 Abram was disillusioned with the gods and I can't blame him. You see, my brother Enlil, myself, all my sons and daughters, all of Enlil's sons and daughters all portrayed ourselves as gods. Our various demands, as you say, "libations", were constant. Abram had enough and decided to leave, so he took his family, countless cattle and sheep and set out on his own. He was by standards back then, a very rich man and was allowed to exercise his free will to leave.

We did not know of Abram's strong will and his need to still be engaged in a belief of the gods. Since Abram was my great great grandchild, his great grandfather Adapa being a son of mine was well versed in our ways and our history.

Therefore after Abram left, and unbeknownst to either Enlil or myself, had fashioned himself a new belief or what you would call a new religion. To a certain extent, Abram had decided the gods were real, there were just too many of them. In his own mind he decided to focus on what deity or deities were most important and fashioned his one true god, Yahweh out of the two most important gods at that time, Enlil and I.

So if you can imagine, the great Yahweh of the Old Testament was simply a mixing of the attributes of Enlil and I that Abram concocted to reduce the multiple demands of many gods down to just one. Since the Adamu were my creation whom I always loved, I became the loving part of Yahweh, while Enlil, always jealous and aggressive, became the avenging or vindictive part of Yahweh.

That is precisely why, when you read your bible, Yahweh is of two minds, one hateful, jealous, vengeful while the other is loving and kind. It is because Abram joined Enlil and myself together into one god that gave rise to what is termed monotheism by melding two into one. In retrospect, it was a practical way for Abram to eliminate the confusion of many gods with many demands to just those of one, even if that one god seemed to have a dual personality and in serious need of psychiatric care.

So Abram set out on his own with his newly minted religion and with a determination to make it true and believable amongst his tribe. I misjudged how prolific and how influential this belief would become. I could have saved many lives over the next 5 millennia had I not let Abram leave Sumeria. As you probably know by now, Sumeria was destroyed by our own means and we Annunaki had to leave Tiamet because of our massive error in judgement.

So everything that you have read in your bible today was written by us about 1500 years previous to when Moses made his first copy. The creation of man by Yahweh was not referring to Yahweh's miraculous act of breathing life into a lump of clay but the simple splicing of genes to give the caveman a reason for being.

The newly created Adamu could not procreate however so we had to clone each new being one by one. It was my son, Ningishzidda who conceived of a method to instil reproductively onto the tree of life of the Adamu. Scientifically speaking, the Adamu when first created only possessed 20 pairs of chromosomes on the DNA strand. When we realized this, Ningishzidda spliced 2 more to make a total of 22 chromosomes thus giving our new creation the ability to reproduce.

Once accomplished, we no longer needed to produce each clone separately and the Adamu could reproduce with the free will mixture of genetic material to begin the propagation of a new race.

As you may imagine, my brother Enlil was furious when he found out. Not so much because he disagreed with the development but that we hadn't informed him or asked permission. My brother was a bit of a dick as you might say today.

Anyway, he was so mad that he expelled the new beings from the medical compound which we had named E.DIN.

After a few generations of procreation, however, the new creatures were of a delightful nature and the females of this new race were magnificent and we began to lay with the females. If you refer to Genesis Chapter 6 you will find that it depicts this event as the sons of god lay with the daughters of men to produce the men of renown.....or something like that. You can see in many other verses how quotes were taken directly from pre-existing Sumerian texts.

However it was my own deed that gave rise to the creation of Adam himself, although he was correctly called Adapa in those days. I sought to prove that the new Adamu had the ability to reproduce with Annunaki. I decided to take part in the experiment myself with two Adamu females in a conjugal manner. I performed the experiment and was delighted to learn 9 months later a boy and girl were born. The boy was named Adapa whom the bible refers to as Adam and the girl was named Tiamet to denote earth mother. You might know her as Eve. Thus, the true lineage of mankind began."

A fly flew into my mouth as my jaw gaped open and dropped to the ground. "This is really hard to believe," I said. "You are describing the creation of man not as the miraculous act of an all powerful god but simply you having sex with a couple of cavewomen."

"Well, I always thought of it as a divine act of procreation," Enki went on to say, "Now the native species were not only advanced into 3rd density by cloning but they would also have the genetics of a superior race as well. Quite a dramatic one-two punch, I might say.

We actually helped to advance Earth along its evolutionary pathway by a few million years. Frankly, we were probably at the same point on the evolutionary scale back then as you are now."

"Evolution, or the concept of evolution has always given me a bad taste," I went on to say. "It's like we came out of the primordial soup 6 billion years ago and evolved by chance from single-celled amoeba to multicellular complex organisms but it's just too far-fetched for me. I say you have to be an idiot to believe that."

"Right," Enki replied. "The fellow you call Charles Darwin popularized that theory about 100 earth years ago and your science community adopted the idea because it brought with it greater ramifications than most people realize."

This was really a test of wills and the battle line was drawn between the new fledgling science community and the well-established and thoroughly entrenched religious one.

Jehovah who supposedly created man was a bastardization of the event which I have just described to you. Most of the Old Testament as you know it in the books that you read today were copied from countless other texts, traditions and verbal translations that predated the bible by about a thousand years.

I had scribes write down many things from when Enlil and I ruled the earth. Marduk did the same when he ushered in the great dynasties of Egypt and Enlil's son Ninurta did the same when he went to what you now call South America to help introduce agriculture and animal husbandry to the people that lived there since this was where Cain had been banished to".

"Whoa, hold on a darn second," I said with more than a little gusto. "I presume we are talking about the Cain and Abel Cain that is featured in Genesis as being the killer of his own brother. Are you saying this is a real event because as far as I was concerned, this was just another mythical story from the bible."

"No," Enki replied. "This was not a mythical story, this was a real story about a real guy named Cain and he shouldn't have killed his brother. It happened almost identically as described in the bible but when it came down to judgement, Enlil and I decided that Cain should be banished, not killed because of a temporary lapse in judgement on his part. He really did deserve another chance to make good and that's exactly what he did. We flew him and his entourage to what you would now call Uruguay in South America where he settled.

Then many years later the great catastrophe happened as described in your ancient texts. The great flood or what we called the deluge did not happen because of Yahweh's judgement of mankind. We had no such power over the forces of nature on this planet. It happened due to a naturally occurring event which involved immense gravitational forces and a close passing.

My home planet Nibiru orbits your sun every 3600 years. Its orbit is like a comet with a very long elliptical path and when the gravitational mass of Nibiru came into proximity with the planets in your solar system, it wreaked havoc. We saw this coming for many years as we knew exactly when our home planet would make its passing. Our instruments showed a great unsettling in the southern polar region of your planet.

When Nibiru neared we hovered above the earth in our vessels and as our home planet passed, the gravitational forces ripped the massive ice sheet from the continent which you now call Antarctica and cast it into the ocean. This created a huge wave which inundated the earth and wiped out almost all of humanity.

The gods had taken council before the event however and since my brother Enlil really did hate our human creation he cast his vote to let all die in the deluge. He convinced many of his family members to vote in accord with his wishes and since he had been declared lord of the earth, he pretty much had the say.

However I got word to my great nephew who you might know as the biblical Noah and instructed him to build a sub-marine like vessel that would house him and his family during the trying time. I also gave him the genetic material to keep safe so that we could recreate many of the beasts that had roamed the land prior to the flood.

Many hundreds of years later Nanurta was sent to check up on the colony which was now in what is called Peru to see if any of Cain's descendants had survived the great flood. Nanurta discovered a remnant of Cain's tribe had survived the disaster in a city high on top of a mountain in Peru which you know today as Maachu Pichu. Nanurta or Quetzalcoatl as he was known to the people of Cain became the great civilizer just as Marduk had done in Egypt."

"That's pretty cool," I said. "A lot of this stuff is really starting to tie together now."

"OK, so let's get back to the theory of evolution as stated by our good friend Charlie Darwin," Enki replied. "Evolution did not quite happen as Chuck envisioned because he was using the scientific method which had been developed by such folk as Isaac Newton many years earlier. He made many assumptions.

On Nibiru, ours was a balanced approach which accounted for both science and spirit. Your development on this planet, which I have been watching closely for about a thousand years now, only looked at what the physical senses provided and did not account for the spiritual. Later on, instruments became an extension of the senses which took humans further away from the realms they needed to so badly balance. That is why Darwin missed the point of evolution because he was unable to take into account the spirit aspect of evolution which of course is the most important part.

We evolve spiritually, not physically, period. In other words, what Charlie saw as a linear progression of increasing complexity from single celled creatures to multiple cells and from invertebrate to vertebrate, fish to amphibian, reptile to bird, animal to ape and ape to human just didn't happen."

"Thank god someone has finally come along to say that the theory of evolution is a big stack of crap," I emphatically replied. "Especially when that someone is a god."

"Well then," Enki replied. "I am filling your brain with a lot of different stuff, but you'll thank me later I'm sure.

Like I was saying, no snake ever became a parrot and no frog ever became an alligator. Second density entities incarnate as second density beings until they are ready to graduate to third density. Third density beings will always incarnate as third density beings until the harvest, then those that are ready will move on to fourth density. And so forth up the so called chain.

Your planet earth started as a first density planet in which the first density entities chose to allow the planet to open up to other beings after a time. The first density entities were earth, air, fire and water and when they were ready, the planet opened up to second density beings. This is when small single-celled creatures first saw an opportunity and were allowed by the primary elements to come in and experience physical life on what had become a second density planet.

This first proliferation of simple life-forms paved the way for more complex forms of second density beings. The planet was set up for these kinds of creatures to develop the necessary experiences so that they could progress. Things like birds, reptiles, mammals and fish were spirit beings manifesting as physical creatures all living simultaneously. Their existence was not separated by vast periods of times as your geologists and archaeologist would suggest. The great reptiles which you call dinosaurs were just another species of life on the planet when all the others were cohabitating across the sphere.

Each new physical life-form was conceived while in spirit. The spirit beings thought all manner of life into existence first as an idea. Then, using the elements available to structure the body, the idea came alive in a myriad of different forms. Some failed some thrived according to the laws of nature that had been established by the first density elements.

The key to understanding this concept however is to realize that all physical beings start first as spirit. When a frog comes into existence on this earth plane, the creature already exists in the spirit realm as an energy essence. The spirit/frog is at a point in its evolution that requires this particular experience as a frog on earth in order to progress. All living things in all parts of the universe are doing the same thing, not just the frog.

Unfortunately, humans have become so arrogant as to devalue the worth of a frog in the scheme of life not realizing that all spring from the same source. In other words we are part of 'All That Is'.

Darwin, and your modern science has become confused mostly because of the introduction of the so-called science of geology which suggest long time periods between findings in the fossil record. It is an assumption they have made which has led them astray and caused this confusion. It is also, a mistake upon your scientific community not to include the spirit aspect. Nibiru was saved from a great calamity because the scientists and spiritualists listened to each other and collaborated.

So there was some progression within species on earth such that horses got bigger with time, dogs became more diverse, apes and chimpanzees developed dexterity to a certain degree but they were always apes. So evolution the way Charles Darwin describes it, just did not happen but I think you already knew this.

What does happen is that animals progress from second density to third density when they are ready and when the time is right. What constitutes the readiness of animals for third density work? First and foremost is the recognition of self. This is the awareness of self and the interaction of self with other selves.

A lion, for example, knows that it is a physical being in a place with other physical beings and is quite a social animal amongst its own. It realizes that it must eat to stay alive so that its interaction with other animals to coordinate the hunt is imperative so that it can kill and eat. It also has a realization that it must procreate in order to propagate the species. When these things become more than instinct and actually become a thought, then the animal becomes a candidate for third density work. Wolves are another good example of this.

Wolves will kill to eat but they will also kill for fun, for the sake of killing. Why? Because they are good at it. They love to kill. Wolves as a pack are not too unlike an early tribe of humans. There is order, there is leadership, there is bravery, and there is lust. The alpha male will always breed the females, why? Not because of Darwin's concept of survival of the fittest but because wolves like humans enjoy screwing. The top dog, sort of speak, gets to impregnate the females because that is his right as biggest and fiercest. The alpha male has fought his way to the top and earned that right.

Now humans know they are distinct beings on a journey of discovery and experience. Where that journey leads, most don't know and religion fills a gap here. For those that are advanced, they realize that religion does not hold all the answers. But like the animal that is seeking to graduate to third density without knowing what that means, the human seeks fourth density without the knowledge of what that means either.

But there are clues and one only needs to keep one's eyes open and ears pricked to get a sense of fourth density because it is there right in front of you. Just like the lion sees the humans in the encampment huddled around the fire and the wolf sees the Indian hunting from afar.

So to, humans sense fourth density by knowing that they exist as a separate entity, knowing that there are other separate entities and that interaction with these other selves is important. Civilized behaviour comes about as a result of this sense of interaction that brings about great advances in discovery of both the world around you and the world inside you.

Then there is this concept of love which nobody really understands and most misunderstand. Most see it as a feeling you may have for another person that is special to you. Love however is the one force in the universe that is all powerful, all-encompassing and contains the secrets of eternal existence. This knowledge doesn't just exist in third density reality. Knowledge of love is not meant for third density. It is meant for intense study in fourth density. The sense of its existence in third density however is the stepping stone to fourth density and that is the sense you get when you have that special feeling for that special person.

That is evolution my friend. A lion knows it must eat but it also realizes that it is part of a much bigger thing going on. Animals can and do sense a richer existence and so they strive to evolve. This is done on an inner level and so a lion will always be a lion for many thousands of years until the spirit of the lion is ready for third density. Then one day the lion will die and a new being will be born ready to experience its existence in the next density.

One of the great questions of your time is how are mass murderers born or nurtured and how is it that some people are natural born killers? They seem to enjoy killing both animals and other humans. Now you know. Some have just transitioned and are still in the early stages of learning how to cope in third density when in fact they have had millions of years of killing and eating and killing in second density.

I should also mention that the earth is a sentient being, one upon which you live and depend upon for life. And like all of you that live here, she is ready to transition again. I told you earlier that the earth was originally a first density planet that transitioned to second density then transitioned to third density. Now the great earth mother is ready to transition again.

The problem has been an intermixing of vastly different types of spirit beings who have chosen to incarnate here and because of this there is no harmony.

So, earthling, I am here to tell you that soon the shit will hit the fan, as the saying goes."

"Enki, that is very ungodlike," I quipped.

Chapter 2: Back home

It was several days later after my encounter with that strange man that I was on a plane back home and after a week had gone by, Hanoi seemed like a distant memory. As for Enki, I wasn't even sure our conversation had happened, as it seemed so surreal. At one point, I even considered it to have been a very lucid dream brought on by too much beer.

It might have even been the goat meat I ate the night before. I chalked it up to "interesting encounters" and left it at that. But in some crazy way, I could not stop thinking about what Enki said and the huge implications it posed, nor his demeanour, disposition or raw conviction.

I considered for a moment that if it were true, the things Enki had shared with me that afternoon in Hanoi, the implications could blow Christianity, Judaism and Darwin's theory of evolution out of the water in one fell swoop. It made me feel like we were the cavemen for believing all the stuff about gods and such.

As I reasoned it through, people mostly do not react to such information in a rational and reasonable way whether it can be proven true or not. Usually the first step taken by rational human beings when something new like this comes to light is to attack the new theory like it was a cancer, something to be feared. Fear of it becoming sensible or reasonable when held up against what is considered true. It was easy to see that Enki's theories were not easily defensible. No devout person or anyone else for that matter would ever stand up and say, hey you're right, how silly of me to have believed all that other crap.

Similarly, what man of science would say, hmm your right, evolution is bullshit. No matter how sensible a new thing is, it is never easily substituted for the old beliefs no matter how ridiculous. I think we were built that way.

The Sumerian clay tablets found in southern Iraq were a huge archaeological discovery but unfortunately they were all jumbled about in sporadic piles amongst the debris, not neatly shelved in chronological order. That probably indicated several chaotic periods between when the tablets were written and when they were discovered.

The only thing more chaotic at this point was all this Enki stuff rattling around in my brain.

Would some ancient civilization play a joke far into the future by writing silly nonsense on a bunch of wet chunks of clay and then giggle themselves all the way to the grave thinking what a great joke it will be when this stuff is dug up in 5000 years.

In most cases historical records are kept by a society or culture, ancient or otherwise to preserve its heritage and create a legacy. There were accurate descriptions of Sumerian societal matters such as, financial doings, legal concerns and government procedures that could only be described if they were in fact utilized and practiced. Was Enki just some crackpot who had studied all this information and was having a good lark?

I suppose, if our world were suddenly to come to an abrupt end and 2000 to 3000 years later an alien civilization of scientists and archaeologists dug up all that was left in the rubble there might be some very interesting conclusions reached.

Perhaps they might come to realize that Harry Potter was a very influential god with special powers, David Banner was the strongest guy that ever lived but only when he got really mad and turned green while the smartest guy was a white faced android named Data. Frankly, it might be hard just to determine who actually existed and who was made up. Time has a funny way of messing things up, I thought to myself.

One interesting aspect of history is that the further we go back in time, the shadier and murkier it gets as to what is true and what is not. I began to think about mythology and how it gets mixed up with the truth. Some read the bible and believe it to be the literal truth front to back as written by men inspired by god.

Yet those same people will read Greek mythology and say that they are made up stories with no shred of truth. I read those same ancient texts and they all seem like myths to me and yet Sitchen's Earth Chronicles reads more like a history text. It's just me I guess but when Lot's wife turns to a pillar of salt for looking back at Sodom and Gomorrah it doesn't seem a whole lot different than when the Medusa turned Ulysses' men to stone when they gazed upon those snaky eyes.

When I read Genesis now, it is like a condensed version of the Sumerian texts. Where the bible says that god made heaven and earth, the Sumerian texts give a lengthy astrological description of earth's creation, the planets and our solar system.

Enki talked about Chapter 6 in the bible and the wickedness of man but wasn't it the sons of god who were lying with the daughters of men?

"When human beings began to increase in number on the earth and daughters were born to them, the sons of god saw that the daughters of humans were beautiful, and they married any of them they chose. Then the Lord said, 'My Spirit will not contend with[a] humans forever, for they are mortal[b]; their days will be a hundred and twenty years. The Nephilim were on the earth in those days— and also afterward—when the sons of God went to the daughters of humans and had children by them. They were the heroes of old, men of renown'.

Who were the Nephilim? Who were the men of renown and why are they mentioned in Genesis.

Sitchen translates the Nephilim as 'those from above' and suggests that it is the Annunaki or the people of Enlil and Enki whom this is in reference to. But then again, it wasn't Sitchen suggesting this, he was only the messenger or translator if you will. It was the Sumerians who made these claims on clay tablets. Maybe Sitchen was wrong in his translation. I had to consider that as well.

What about the tower of Babel and the strange wording that exists in Genesis Chapter 11, "But the Lord came down to see the city and the tower the people were building. The Lord said, "If as one people speaking the same language they have begun to do this, then nothing they plan to do will be impossible for them. Come, let us go down and confuse their language so they will not understand each other."

I wondered why the great and powerful Yahweh, creator of the universe, should be concerned about the abilities of man and why he needed to confer with others to go down and confuse the language.

What was really going on here such that the great Jehovah would be afraid of men? Where did he come down from? Were the Babylonians fixin' for a fight?? Why not wave his almighty hand to fix everything from wherever he was. I can surely order a beer with no less effort. In other situations the bible describes the Lord raining down fire from heaven to destroy men and whatnot. Why not do it in this case?

A modern day translation of this biblical event might read, "Hey boys, finish your beers and then let's go down to Babel and mess up those sum biches. They think they know everything, so let's show 'em a thing or two. They're gonna get what's comin to em."

The Sumerian account of this event, which predates the bible, has pages and pages (or pieces of clay after pieces of clay) of descriptions entailing what we read as an act of arrogance and aggression by Enki's son Marduk and in fact it was Enlil who put a stop to it. It was actually Enlil who was afraid of what Marduk may have accomplished and even today, Marduk is known as the ancient Babylonian god. And so it all starts to make sense with Enki suggesting that Yahweh was invented by Abram to synthesize him and Enlil into one supreme god. It was surely a credible theory, I thought.

Then immediately upon thinking that thought, I thought another thought that had me thinking I was truly crazy for thinking that thought.

Since I had been a Christian most of my life I began to wonder about when Jesus came along some 2000 years after Abram made his departure from Ur. It was confusing in that Yahweh was clearly a god of war who ordered mass murders and other dubious acts in direct contrast to the teaching of love and self-sacrifice that Jesus proffered.

If Jesus had been at his father Jehovah's side when he issued the order for Joshua to enter the land of Canaan and kill every man, woman and child then maybe Jesus would have been jumping up and down yelling whoa pops, let's think about this for a second. It might have sounded like a conversation George Sr. had with George W prior to bombing the crap out of Iraq. Come on George, let's go down and shock and awe them Canaanites. Hmm.

But the rationalization was loud and clear, at least in my head anyway. Sadaam Hussein was evil and needed to be dealt with. The Canaanites were evil as well and they could not go unpunished.

So the debate raged on in my head until one day my wife and I happened to a walk through a park in the central city core where we lived and lo and behold there was a fare in progress.

Off to one side a big sign over one of the booths read "Jesus Saves" and this became like a beacon to me. I always seem to gravitate towards these things whether it's Christian, Mormon or Jehovah's Witness. My wife used to always laugh when the Hare Krishna's were around because, for some strange reason, they always tried to get me to join. But this booth was drawing me in like a moth to a big old spot light so I had to investigate.

It was not long before I struck up a conversation with a young woman who immediately said that god had a plan for me. This bothered me for some reason. Perhaps he did but this young woman saying he did was not a convincing argument. How did she know that god had a plan for anyone let alone one for me? In fact Enki had been much more convincing in what he had shared with me that day in Hanoi.

But who was right? This woman with a book and 4000 years of history or Enki and his wild ass story and 5000 years of history.

That got me thinking about Enki in comparison to the young woman in front of me. Both had put themselves out there as an authority in the doctrine they firmly believed. The young woman kept looking up to the sky, Tim Tebow fashion as if receiving inspiration from god himself, or so it seemed. Enki looked me directly in the eye, searching for a glimmer of understanding in mine. He would say his piece and then pause to let me absorb and then ask questions where needed. Our conversation was an ebb and flow of thoughts and ideas trading back and forth. With this young woman, it was repetition and a skyward flick of the eyes.

"God has a plan for you my friend", chirped the young woman as she flicked her eyes to the heavens still yet another time.

"Thanks for that", I replied, "But it's not me that I am worried about. You see I have a friend in Pakistan whose girlfriend was raped by a group of men from the next village and since the authorities determined it was her fault for dressing inappropriately, she is scheduled to be stoned to death. What is god's plan for her?" I asked.

"God works in mysterious ways", she replied looking up as if asking for heavenly protection from my evil influence.

Was that all she had to offer? Who was I to believe, a young seemingly sane woman with the dedication to a belief that was part history and part myth, or an eloquent middle-aged European man with steely blue eyes and a penchant for a good story. Could it be that one was a lunatic while the other was telling a compelling truth? I just didn't know which was which.

At that point, I was resigned to believe that intellectually, I was not about to get much more in the way of explanation from the young Christian woman than what I had already received. So I flicked my eyes heavenward, dusted off my sandals and continued on my journey not even bothering to tell her that I had made up the story about the poor girl in Pakistan. The really sad thing about it was the story might have been true.

I was chuckling to myself upon reflection of the encounter with the young woman while my wife, who somehow always seemed to endure my silliness, was bristling.

"Can't help it," I said.

"You need help," was her curt reply.

"Yes, I know, I'm a dick."

The park was crowded and as we walked, the bright sun warmed our faces as I reflected upon the recent conversations. Then, as we walked past a bench, there sat a man that caused me to turn completely around as I could have sworn it was Enki, my friend from Hanoi, but it wasn't, just someone who looked like him.

I never told anyone about my conversation with Enki. On several occasions I had brought up the Earth Chronicles by Zecharia Sitchen to friends as a matter of casual conversation which was always met with the same stare of incredulity. I thought maybe I had grown horns on my forehead and certainly the young girl in the park probably thought I was the second cousin to Satan himself.

This caused me to think that Christianity and Enkianity maybe weren't all that different. I knew that Christianity had undergone major changes from its original form and that many things had been written in later on.

I knew that the gospels were written some 100 years after Jesus' death, 3 of the 4 anyway. Mark was written about 35 years afterwards so it would be easy to insert, modify and edit things in those ensuing years.

I knew that the council of Nicaea in 345 AD was to determine if Jesus was divine or not. I wondered why it took 345 years to figure out that he was divine. That was if he really was divine.

I had the sense that Jesus said many important things during his time on Earth like how we as humans need to live in harmony and we are much more than we see ourselves to be.

From my own background as a Christian having grown up in the church, reading and studying the bible I was quite aware of the disconnect between the Old Testament and the new. In fact it had occurred to me that if I ever wanted to dissuade anyone from becoming a Christian I would tell them to read the Old Testament.

I would tell them to read Genesis, Numbers, Deuteronomy and Joshua just to get a sense of The Lord, Jehovah, Yahweh, Elohim, El Shaddam or whatever it was that he called himself. Lots of different names for the same fellow but then to have him pose as the almighty creator of the universe and Jesus' dear ol' dad was becoming a bit of a stretch for me. There was no harmony being sought by Jehovah, just death and destruction.

Enki crafted a story too. His basis was essentially what was written on the clay tablets excavated from various sites determined to be ancient Sumerian cities. The story was based on Enki and his people coming from another planet within our solar system where that planet has a much different orbit that cannot be detected by modern science.

Enki's existence could not be proven any more than could Jesus' or Jehovah. It was all circumstantial and the things that Enki had accomplished were no more provable than Jesus walking on the Galilee or ordering fish and chips for 5000.

The obvious difference, it seemed, was that Enki, or whoever he was, was sitting with me flesh and blood while Jesus wasn't. Quite an advantage if one was crazy enough to believe that Enki was Enki. Apparently Jesus existed 2000 years ago and there are lots of people who take that as the truth.

But to me Christianity was still plausible even if it was becoming difficult to sort through all the inconsistencies. I understood that most things that have happened in the past take a certain amount of faith in order to believe that history got it right. I also don't believe everything I'm told just because someone says it's true.

Enki, on the other hand, was quite easy to disbelieve as most of what he was saying was some of the craziest shit I had ever heard yet what he was saying made some kind of demented sense. Believing or disbelieving does not change what is true. But having a belief drilled into your head from childhood is just plain brainwashing in my mind.

 You haven't got a chance in breaking free from a belief if the belief was instilled from birth and honed during the formative years. To me, it didn't matter what the belief was, be it Judaism or communism. One should be able to accept or reject these things under free will conditions.

My wife would argue that one should teach children and then let them choose for themselves as adults what to believe or not believe. But how come there were so many people that never challenged the beliefs they were taught as children? Why were there so many beliefs?

 I did not consider myself a lunatic or a crazed religious person handing out pamphlets on the street corner but I was not really fully engaged in any particular belief either.

For some people it never entered their minds that there could be something else to consider that would constitute a new paradigm especially if it meant leaving the church.

For others, it took courage to leave the church. Often the direct result of some kind of upheaval in their life.

Yet for others it was a slow easy drift away. Just like floating down the river on a hot sunny afternoon with a cooler full of cold beer. In other words, not traumatic at all.

For me, I was an inbetweener. I didn't get too serious about too much of anything. Maybe a better word for it was lazy. There were the 7 disciplines of Buddhism and the 5 Pillars of Islam or was it the other way around. Either way, it seemed like a lot of work. The Origin of Species was exhausting to read and equally exhausting to believe.

I didn't want to be a nihilist either because there was no fun in that. You had to believe in something even if it's left of center socialism like in Canada or really to the left like communism in Vietnam. Being inbetween all of the stuff out there was fine by me.

Maybe I didn't need to know everything about what life was about right away. If there was an alternative that makes sense, I guess I would know soon enough. Patience.

I think that devout Christians are Christian because they are terrified. I was terrified because God says I will be condemned if I stop believing. There is no one to protect me against the principalities of evil and worst of all, there is no one to guarantee eternity. To face eternity without the right belief you could face the fires of eternal torment. Who wants that?

I was an inbetweener because I really didn't think too much about that whole heaven and hell thing. I really considered it to be scare tactics aimed at the medieval folk during the dark ages.

Maybe Christianity was more like an insurance policy than a religion. We believe in God because we mostly need protection from all the nasty things that can happen in life. We honour and praise God because we basically want something from him.

 Just like when your house burns down, the insurance company compensates the individual for the cost of building a new one. If your uncle dies, God insures that he has a new life in heaven. Even if Uncle George was a mean cantankerous old son-bitch, the good padre would say that Uncle George was in heaven with God. We all want it to be true but I was just never sure that it was.

So God becomes an insurance policy for the afterlife, after all, insurance companies here on earth will insure death but they will not insure the afterlife. God will however, insure the afterlife by setting up a nifty program that makes it easy, you just have to believe.

Even though I considered myself to be an inbetweener, it still comforted me that there might be a nice place up there for me to go when I die. Maybe I could get on a slo-pitch team. One that wasn't too serious about winning games but liked having beers after the game instead. Maybe even play some hockey if The Lord had ice somewhere.

The point that was becoming clear in my mind was that fear prevents most level headed, intelligent human beings from thinking rationally. If you had been a practicing Christian since childhood with beliefs instilled by your parents from an early age coupled with a pious reverend espousing from the pulpit how God loves you then it becomes a massively powerful one-two punch and absolutely terrifying to contemplate the alternative of giving it up.

The simple reality of the Christian religion was to make everyone believe they are flawed. Show people that when they are held up to an all-powerful being that is all good, we are but scum in comparison. Show people that there is a fix and it is simple.

That was the attraction for me, the simplicity of it.

Most Christians see the alternative to Christianity as some other religion such as Islam, Hinduism or Buddhism and that these are all flawed whereas Christianity isn't. It suggests that ongoing adherence to the idea portrayed in a series of books written 2000 years ago is somehow grounds for proof.

I never accepted the bible as proof of anything. To me it was simply a collection of stories. That never seemed to dissuade me from my belief in Jesus as being a great teacher.

Atheism is the one big scientifically based alternative that presents itself as another way to look at life, but personally, I always thought it was rather depressing. When you die, everything goes black and you simply cease to exist – outstanding.

We are only here by the chance occurrence of atoms and molecules arranging themselves in a pattern that brought about life in the primordial soup billions of years ago? The diversity and complex progression of life arose from genetic mutations and survival of the fittest?

I never thought of Charles Darwin in the same light as Jesus Christ.

Giving up Christianity for Darwinism would be like telling your mom that you have finally given up smoking by replacing it with heroin.

Chapter 3: A reintroduction

It had been really tough after my return from Vietnam. Maybe not as tough as the guys coming back in the 70's but work was scarce and the big projects seemed to be avoiding me as if they had a mind of their own. Several small ones had come along but thank goodness my wife had a good steady job that put bread on the table for us. The odd beer as well I might add.

As part of our morning routine, I would walk with my wife to work and we would sit with friends and have coffee before everyone went off to their respective offices. I would stay and read the paper then later walk back home and work on my projects.

As I was reading the paper one rainy day and dreading the walk back home in the drizzle when a man walked up and asked if he could sit. Without looking up, I recognized the voice and instantly knew it was my friend from Hanoi.

"Hello Enki," I said even before I peered above my newspaper whilst sipping my coffee. "I wasn't sure if I would ever see you again, or if you were just a daytime dream that I had in some sort of humid, alcohol induced state."

"Ha, ha," he replied sarcastically. "I've been called many things over the ages but never a shit-faced booze phantom. Besides it's nice to see you again."

"I hadn't quite meant it like that," I replied sheepishly. "Forgive me, but I am surprised to see you. What may I ask are you doing here in this shabby town?"

"I am on a mission from god," he jokingly replied (which was one of my favourite quotes from the Blues Brothers and somehow I got the feeling from the look in his eyes that he knew this). Actually I am on a mission but it's a little different than usual I guess. Humankind hangs in the balance, and I am here to help with the tipping point sort of speak."

"Well, you are never short of surprises," I replied. "First you tell me that you are a Sumerian god, now you are back to save the world. You're not one to mince words nor do you suffer from a lack of self-esteem, so tell me more about this world saving stuff but be warned, I am still having a tough time with the whole god thing and I have my bullshit-O-meter with me."

I was taking a chance in saying that especially if he really was a god but sometimes you just got to have some fun.

"Look," he said. "It was your ancestors that elevated me and my brother to god status. We came to realize that our interference was massive, in many ways bad and in some ways good. Ultimately, had we not showed up and interfered with your genetics and evolutionary timeline, you would just be crawling out of some cave right about now. You would be the missing link."

"Where are woman to drag by hair. Ugh. Me make fire."

"Yes, well, back to why I am here. As you know there is a lot of talk of end times and whether Tiamet and those who live on her surface will cease to exist. Nobody seems to know and there is much confusion.

Your movies depict this event, religious texts have always talked about end times and even the Mayan calendar suggested the end in 2012 after nearly 5000 years keeping track of time. The world as you know it is coming to an end, but not in a way that any of you can imagine. I am here to help out and give clarity on the issues at hand. Nothing ends without also ushering in a new beginning."

"I have to tell you Enki," I interrupted. "I was going to go home and chill in front of the tube and watch some golf but you have again captured my attention so please continue."

"Tiamet," he continued. "Is going through a transition and I have been sent to help with the changes. I was chosen as a representative of the Annunaki people to interact with humans in these end times to help with the understanding of change. Why the Annunaki, why me, you might ask? Because of our experience of going through the same changes that you face and my direct influence in altering human genetics".

"Enki," I replied. "I have heard of all that junk about end times before. We have had wacko religious guys preaching certain dates for the world to end for ages and none of them have ever happened. We all thought something crazy would happen on Dec. 31, 1999 but the world went on. Then Dec. 21, 2012 came and went, nothing happened and the world continued as usual."

"This is the problem," he replied. "Everyone expects a pinpoint placement of time for one major catastrophic event to occur. Then there is the expectation that those who wake up the next morning find themselves in a world that looks like The Matrix, Mad Max or The Terminator. People need to understand that changes, small and large, subtle or gross have been occurring over a longer period of time which is leading to a "phasing in" event.

This is not a spectacularly catastrophic event but one that started approximately 25 years ago and will continue to occur for another 50 - 100 years, maybe more.

Consider all the major events in your world for the past 3 decades such as wars, financial meltdowns, moral upheavals' and crazy weather patterns. Consider these as birth pains. Global warming is the best example of what I am talking about. When a person is sick, they sometimes burn up with fever, or when a woman is giving birth, there is someone to help dissipate the heat with a cool cloth. The earth mother is giving birth to a new world and I am here to help apply the cool cloth."

I was fascinated by the idea that global warming was not man-made or induced by man's activities but merely a pregnant mother getting ready to give birth.

"Are you saying," I continued. "That global warming is not man-made."

"Of course it isn't", Enki replied. "The earth mother is alive and well and she is a very powerful being. Do you and your fellow man really think that you can affect change to an extent as to cause the earth mother unwanted duress? Do you think that your small factories and your piddly little transportation pods could produce a damaging effect to cause the great mother pain?

It is within her power to get rid of all of you like a flea off a dog's back. The deluge wiped out all of mankind in a matter of days and all your ancient records show this to be true. It would only take 3 Krakatau's or 4 Mt. St. Helens erupting at once to inundate the world with a sky-blackening ash ushering in a 100-year winter which would wipe out nine-tenths of the population in one year.

In other words, natural disasters translate into earth mother's will. She can do as she pleases. All 7 billion people present on this planet are here because she desires it. You all desire it too, it's just that you know nothing about what is taking place.

How arrogant earth people have become to think you cause global warming. When Ningishzidda and I fashioned the first Homo sapiens we saw great potential and great humility which was inherent in the DNA. That was 6000 years ago but as time progressed mankind grew in knowledge and understanding but most of all, man grew in his delusion and arrogance."

I could see that Enki was getting a little hot under the collar so I changed the subject by saying, "Tell me what the Mayans were trying to measure if it wasn't the end of the world?"

"But of course," he replied. "When your calendar comes to the date December 31 what does it signify?"

"A year has gone by?"

"Right, it denotes the completion of one revolution of the earth around the sun. That was what the Mayans were measuring, one revolution of your solar system around the central galactic sun. Nothing more."

"OK, this is pretty easy to understand but still the Mayan calendar means something more than that, right?"

"Yes it does. Five revolutions represent one period or 25,000 of your years. And 3 of these periods are required for the age to be completed. Your world is coming up to the end of the 75,000 year cycle as measured by the Mayans in 5,000 year increments. Your apocalyptic writings point to the new age through clues on what will happen and what it will look like. Jesus tried to portray this in an eloquent fashion but his words were greatly distorted."

"OK, now we are getting somewhere," I said. "I know what the present world looks like. It's crappy. People killing other people and all that, so tell me what the new age is supposed to look like. I get that the transitionary period is long and drawn out as opposed to a single catastrophic event but at some point the changes will be accomplished. At that point the world should look different, don't you think."

"Nobody in my realm really knows but I can tell you what it might look like based on what we experienced on my home world about 2000 earth years ago. When we left your planet after the terrible destruction brought about by our own infighting, a mistake we regret to this day. Enlil, I and the other Annunaki went back to our home planet Nibiru where we were greeted and honoured as heroes returning from a great battle.

Not long after however, our world began to heat up and our scientists determined that the volcanic activity that had stopped centuries earlier had begun again. Since our mission to Tiamet was to gather gold to be sent back to Nibiru to be made into fine dust for distribution into the atmosphere to preserve heat, our mission was successful. But with volcanic activity started again, the golden atmosphere imprisoned us on a planet that would eventually roast us all to death.

That was the science talking and our scientists were very accurate in their assessment. But we Annunaki gave equal merit to the spirit advisors and they determined that the great mother was giving birth and it was our time for transition.

The huge difference between what we went through and what you are going through is that we were a unified, informed people, balanced in the things that were technical and spiritual. There were no false beliefs brought about by various religious teachings and multiple philosophies confusing the matter. We were much further advanced on the evolutionary scale and better prepared for the change.

We saw ourselves as one, acted as one, thought as one which culminated in cooperation, compassion and understanding throughout our transition. But more importantly, we understood that the planet we lived on was a living sentient being that was also in transition.

Therefore, we made the transition en masse, planet and all, from 3rd density to 4th density with little strife. Plus, we had the added benefit of realizing what the nature of the changes were before they happened. For the most part earth people do not have a clue to what is happening and you are confused by a multitude of conflicting beliefs."

"How, if you don't mind my asking, did you and the rest of your comrades survive the planet heating up as I assume that it continued to do so?"

"You're right, Nibiru continued to increase in temperature, but our transition to 4th density changed the nature of our bodies. Hot and cold was no longer an issue as it had been in 3rd density.

All the people on Nibiru had a deep understanding of the cycle of ages. Even our children knew and understood what most of the people on Earth have never heard of. That is the cycle of ages that takes place on all planets in all solar systems in all galaxies throughout the universe.

It is the most important time cycle to be aware of as it determines the next level of spiritual evolution that the population is ready to embrace. We knew as our planet heated up that we were headed into a golden age and that the transition to 4th density was near.

No one knew when it would happen but we patiently waited while the necessary planetary changes took place that would support our newly reincarnated bodies.

Earth, on the other hand, was populated from many other areas of the galaxy but also included the indigenous population that we genetically modified. That is why you see so much strife and discord on your planet. The people on earth differ greatly from each other not only on a cellular level but also spiritually. Great portions of your population are negatively polarized and that is why there is so much confusion."

Enki paused and looked at me with a quizzical stare as if waiting for me to ask about the new concept he had just introduced. Frankly, I was flabbergasted and had no idea what to ask, what to say, what to believe or what the hell was going on. My brain felt like a package of Sapporo Ichiban that had just been boiled for 2 minutes.

I didn't know what to ask because I was still pondering the 3rd density to 4th density thing, then the question suddenly leaped into my head in a way that startled me. It was like someone had tied the question to an arrow and shot it into the side of my head. I think my skull actually bounced a bit when it hit.

"OK," I said. "Let's come back to the density thing in a bit but now you are talking about a negatively polarized part of earth's population. Naturally if there is a negative then there must also be a positively polarized portion as well. Would you kindly fill me in on what you mean by positive and negative polarization?"

"I thought you would never ask," he smiled. "But first let me give you a little background so that you can understand the concept better. Humans are like all other 3rd density beings in the universe. You are made up of mind/ body/spirit. When I first encountered the humanoid species many eons ago you were an ape-man or what I have described as a caveman. This shows in your fossil records seen today and your scientists aptly named you Cro-Magnon man. A sister species which existed around the same time was called Neanderthal man. These we regarded as 2nd density creatures, same as the true apes and same as other mammals that existed at that time. All were second density forms of life and not ready yet for transition to 3rd density.

When my sister Ninmah and I started our experiment to produce a worker species using this existing caveman as a start, we had no idea that we were providing the vehicle to change a 2nd density being into 3rd by what you now call genetic engineering.

In other words, splicing our own genetic material onto this humanoid's tree of life gave the new species, which you call Homo sapien, the ability of the mind. The new species then became mind/body/soul entities which up until then, 2nd density beings were body/soul only. The animal kingdom, which is a 2nd density domain, operates on instinct not thought.

"Wait, just hold on a second," I interrupted. "This makes no sense to me. Give me some baseline, talk to me about why this was happening and what was the driving need for a worker race to have mind/body/soul. Wouldn't you want to keep the workers strong and dumb? Maybe like robots or something."

"On the contrary, we wanted to have a worker capable of thought so that simple instructions could be carried out. I also had an inkling that we were embarking on something very important so let me now quote your bible:

 "In the beginning God created the heavens and the earth. Now the earth was formless and empty, darkness was over the surface of the deep, and the Spirit of God was hovering over the waters".

This statement you can take as being important. But first let me say there were many different names for God in the Hebrew language. He went by El, El Shaddam, El Eyron, Yahweh and Jehovah. All of these names were translated in English to The Lord or The Lord God. It is "The One Infinite Creator" or "All That Is" that is being referenced in the first verse. After that, the god referenced in what you call the Old Testament was simply one of the many war gods of the ancient world. I'll explain more about this later. Then somewhere around Exodus Ch: 6 The Lord who in Hebrew is called El Shaddam decides to change his name to Yahweh. This was where Enlil came in and took up the mantle of God to impress Moses. Do you get it? God in the first verse differs vastly than god who is referred to as Yahweh thereafter. God in the first verse we call "The One Infinite Creator" and even the Annunaki acknowledge. The One Infinite Creator is the creator and benefactor of all that is. Yahweh was just my brother.

So let's step away from the earth, earth history and religion for the moment. All That Is does not give one hoot about religion, worship, acknowledgment or anything else. All That Is creates and experiences itself through what it has created. He is the creator and the created all at the same time.

This forms the backdrop for what you were asking a moment ago; how this fits together. Humans have forgotten a very important aspect of who they are. Some humans think that there is a heaven and hell with a big overruling god that judges and determines where they will spend the rest of eternity. You think you are born once then off you go, up to heaven or down to hell.

There could be nothing further from the truth. Religious thought alone has been disastrous for men and women alike for thousands of years as it limits freedom and confines creative thought. Think of your period in history called the "dark ages" and then realize what caused this to occur. It occurred because there was a coincident rise of a major world religion called Christianity. I can tell you from a position of knowledge and authority that one begat the other. Christianity brought forth the dark times of ignorance and misunderstanding.

But some humans today think that there is no god at all and their ancestors were born in the primordial soup billions of years ago then molded by the unintelligent forces of nature and genetic mutation. This is a fabrication as well.

Humans are immortal beings and they haven't a clue as to the infinite power they possess. A human life of about 80 years is but the blink of an eye in the total conscious existence of the energy essence that is you. Your existence on this planet is based on an illusion you call reality. This so-called reality is a learning ground for your development. Listen carefully since what I will say is true and you need to understand this completely.

You choose to exist in this illusion you call life. You choose to learn, grow and develop here as mind/body/souls. Ultimately when you die, you transition back to who you really are......an infinite being of immense proportion on a journey of self-discovery and value fulfilment.

While you are in body form on earth you create your reality. Once you realize this you can take responsibility for everything that happens to you and the world around you. You created it and if you are listening to me and truly hear what I am saying then you must realize that you are All That Is. Every human, me and all Annunaki, all things in all creation are All That Is.

Even though you live for approximately 80 years, the entity that you are, will always be in existence, forever. You have always been alive and will always be alive and yet you do not realize this.

The very short game that you play on earth as 3rd density beings is only a small part of your existence and you are here to learn and evolve but most important of all, you must realize you are a part of All That Is and he is a part of you. This was what Jesus meant when he said, "I am in the father and the father is in me". He meant that for us all not just himself. The father he was referring to obviously wasn't Yahweh but the One Infinite Creator or All That Is.

You as humans would have eventually arrived where you are as 3rd density creatures sooner or later but if it wasn't for our interference, you would be graduating from 2nd to 3rd density instead of getting ready for 4th.

I thought I was creating a worker species but in reality I created a god; you. I didn't know that at the time but I know it now.

So you play a small game on a small planet for a small period of time in order to grow and seek fulfilment. However, a curious aspect of the game is what we call "the veil" and is used to forget who you are. By doing this you play the game more effectively. Each situation on earth that you encounter no matter how small, how large, how pleasant or how devastating is just a passing event in a very small portion of your existence.

Your most important reason for cycling through multiple lives on earth is to determine your polarity for moving forward into the next density. You see, you must define your path back to the Creator and you define that by declaring your actions as being positively orientated or negatively orientated.

Since we are all on a journey back to the One Infinite Creator, we declare how we will make that journey while in 3rd density. That is what it's all about and that is why it is so important for humans to understand. There is a choice to be made. The choice comes after cycling through 75,000 years of incarnations in 3rd density to choose how you will proceed to 4th density and beyond."

"Enki, awhile back you were going to define for me this idea of positive polarity versus negative polarity", I interceded. "If you are telling me that this choice defines how we will spend the next billions years, then it's pretty important to know what that means."

"Very well", he said. "A positively polarized person is one that lives his/her life as a loving, compassionate, generous person who thinks of others, helps others and serves others. These people are kind, gentle, forgiving and very easy to get along with. They sometimes get pushed around because of their gentle nature and find it difficult when there is a confrontation or heated argument. They are looked upon as meek, mild and easily persuaded. It is best to describe these people as loving and nurturing but unfortunately they are also described as weak. To sum up, this is a person who seeks to serve others. These people are usually caregivers, doctors, nurses or mid to lower level employees in the service industry.

One of the most highly advanced souls on the earth today works as a waitress at a 24-hour truck stop in Nevada.

Negatively polarized people are those that seek to control, manipulate and dominate others. They seek to serve themselves in all manner and ways possible but mostly by enslaving others to their ideas, way of thinking and actions. These people can be seen as nasty and mean on the inside while smiling and cooperative on the outside. They want to be in charge and dominate others, control situations and put people in their rightful place which is always below themselves. They can best be described as forceful, vengeful, arrogant and narcissic. To sum up, these are people who seek to serve themselves. These people often find themselves in position of authority as they work extremely hard to get there. Military leaders, CEO's, head coaches, pastors and just about anyone who has people below them in some fashion would be considered as being negatively polarized.

The degrees of negativity go up as you climb the corporate ladder such that mid-level managers are less negatively polarized than vice-presidents who are in turn less than the CEO or Chairman of the Board.

Same goes with the military but the interesting one is the Catholic church. Priests are less negative than bishops who are less than cardinals who are less than the most negatively polarized person in the church.....guess who."

"The pope," I surmised.

"Yes, well done, the Pope. The one person on the face of the earth who has disguised himself so well and so completely that no one would ever suspect that he and his predecessors are in the same class as the great military leaders throughout history.

But there is no judgement on the part of All That Is, as to how a mind/body/soul entity chooses to polarize as he is only interested in experiencing all things through his creation. All beings are making their way back to the One Infinite Creator and there are only two paths to take and 3rd density is the place of choosing.

This opens up the possibility that there is no such thing as good and evil. You must now consider that this is just an earth concept that exists nowhere else in the universe. There is only positive polarity and negative polarity and I will leave you to ponder this concept.

The problem is that Homo sapien does not know this and therefore, men and women alike go about their many existences missing what's important. Polarity, my friend, polarity is what you are here for – to define your path back to the One Infinite Creator. This defines your path from 3rd density right through to 7th density which if I was to estimate this in terms of your earth time, would represent 15 million years. So you might want to get it right."

"OK, I get that part," I said. "But why? Why polarize, why go through all of this pain and suffering just to make a decision?"

"It's not just about making a decision but defining a pathway. And it's not just defining a pathway but experiencing all things along the path. The idea of polarities came about as an experiment. Let me back up a bit and explain.

When the One Infinite Creator decided to create she created what I will call Logos. Logos created sub-Logos and sub-Logos created sub-sub-Logos. But there was no hierarchy in creation since the Creator was in all Logos and Logos in all sub-Logos and sub-Logos in all sub-sub-Logos. In fact there is no part of creation in which the Creator is not experiencing itself as both the created and the creator. This means that you are the Creator as am I.

The one infinite Creator first contemplated infinity. From infinity the first Logoi burst forth as a thought from the One Infinite Creator. These were the central galactic suns, all of them. Then the thought that gave rise to the Logos also gave rise to other suns and galaxies. Your scientists saw evidence of this in the heavens and postulated the Big Bang Theory where all matter seems to be ever expanding from one central point.

We, the Annunaki saw this as well but probably 2 million years before your Stephen Hawking first proposed the theory. Be that as it may, the One Infinite Creator in his infinite wisdom and with a single thought, burst forth into existence all that is and allowed the first Logoi the same creative capacity as herself.

The Logoi, in the same capacity as the Creator created the sub-Logoi which encompassed all the stars in the sky including what you call the central sun of your own solar system and the countless billions of other suns and planetary systems. The sun then, a sub-Logos and a sentient being, carried on the work of creation using its vast energy to create sub-sub Logoi and that, my dear friend, is where you fit in. You are a son of the sun or as Jesus tried to teach before it was grossly distorted, the son of the One Infinite Creator.

He was really trying to say that we are the sons of the sun therefore it would seem fitting that the ancient sun-worshipping cultures were closer to the truth than any of your modern religions today except for one important point. The sub-logos or sun couldn't give a damn if you realize this or not. The sun, like All That Is, creates to experience itself in its creation. It creates and sets in motion experiments of creation and then collaborates with other sub-Logoi to share information. The sun at the center of your solar system created the system that you experience today. It was this sun that created the veil as an experiment."

"OK, OK, let's talk about the veil. You are telling me, I think, there were other systems in play where polarity and choice were not issues and there was no veiling or forgetting either. What did those worlds look like and what was the reason for the change? It seems to me that peace, freedom, no worries, no killing, none of the atrocities that we see today existed in these other worlds because they had the benefit of knowing who they were, a hologram of the creator himself, herself or whatever."

"Right, all would have been good except there was no progress either, there was no evolution of the mind, body or spirit. Imagine a poker game in which you know what cards the other players are holding as well as your own. You cannot make progress in the game nor is it fun since you already know the outcome. Is the game captivating or invigorating? Is there tension and excitement? Pretty soon you would become bored and lose interest.

In this current system of which you are a part, you are formed in the fire, moulded and shaped by the very challenges and problems that you face. You don't know what the cards are and you certainly don't know it is a game that you have created for yourself. You have set the harsh conditions for yourself.

The Mayan long count calendar was based on a 25,000-year cycle which they measured 5000 years at a time. Every 3rd 25,000-year cycle or 75,000 of your revolutions around the sun, there is a graduation or harvest that takes place. The graduation is for those who are ready for 4th density work. Those who are not ready remain in 3rd density and continue to work until the next harvest.

In previously unveiled situations, entities could still make a choice concerning transition but they knew that they were playing a game. Mind/body/spirit complexes simply incarnated in 3rd density for cycle after cycle with no desire for progress and therefore did not make any choice. The game was played again and again with no stress, no challenge and therefore no development or progress. It was easy, like being on holidays so the entities simply did not move forward because they knew it was a game and it was fun. They made their lives exciting since free will was intact and creation of their lives was a choice.

It makes a huge difference when you choose how to make progress when in spirit as opposed to in body. When the Spirit incarnates and remembers, it tends to change its original plan and take the easy road. When Spirit incarnates and forgets, it follows through with its plan because it forgets the difficult task it has set.

The ultimate game for all creation is to move on a path towards the One Infinite Creator. During this journey each and every one of us combine our experiences as co-creators to join and share our vast experiences in one big multiple millennium party. It can occur in an infinite number of ways and it was pondered that a new way may be beneficial.

Your own sub-Logos realized this salient point and devised the experiment of a veiled choice which is what you enjoy today. The evolutionary progress has been stunning to say the least. Spirits soar as each incarnation builds upon the last and amazing progress is made one poverty-stricken incarnation after another, one rich and famous incarnation after another.

One incarnation is easy, another difficult. One harbours disaster after disaster while another is happiness and bliss and yet others are combinations thereof. This is how you learn and evolve and this is why the veil is important but there comes a time when the veil is no longer needed.

Fourth density work no longer requires the veil and as you approach fourth density you should sense this. Those requiring more work in 3rd density will not understand these concepts and continue to forget. Now, let me show you your illusion."

Chapter 4: The Illusion

His words were like someone had slapped me upside the head and I literally got out of my seat without knowing I had gotten up. I had been half mesmerized by the barrage of information that Enki had been spewing forth.

He talked quickly and there was so much to absorb that the words felt like they were little ping-pong balls rattling around inside my head, bouncing off the bone. Rather thick bone I might add. More like each ball was an idea or thought rather than a collection of words tied together in sentences. I would find out afterwards that something was very different in my ability to retain information.

I stood at attention waiting for Enki's next words.

"We are going for a walk and I will show you your illusion", Enki said with a smile on his face. "I will show you how you are fooled by your own game."

"Where are we going," I asked innocently.

"Doesn't matter," he snapped back. "Just walk, listen to my words and follow my instructions."

"Of course," I replied smugly.

Enki stopped in his tracks, turned and narrowed his eyes at me.

"Now listen to me carefully."

Just as he said those words, I felt a sharp blow across the back of my shoulders.

"Hey," I responded, quite surprised.

"Now, I want you to chant the following: EL-KA-LEEM-OHM, as close in pronunciation and tone as I just said. Do you need me to repeat?"

"Oh come on Enki," I complained. "I will not walk around a downtown metropolitan city chanting some archaic Sumerian saying which probably means kick me cause I'm an idiot."

"This is a chant to the four sacred elements, earth, air, fire and water, who by the way are first density entities and were first to inhabit this sphere. The words I have given you provide the closest phonetic verbalization your language allows, but you don't have to do it at all if you don't want, I am merely helping you understand the lessons I have come to teach."

"OK, I will do your little chant, but if some Sumerian guy comes up to me and wants to know why I am calling his mother a whore, I will not be happy. In other words, this better not be a joke. Now how did that chant go?"

"EL-KA-LEEM-OHM.

It must be said exactly like that. When you speak it, try to keep a feeling of gratitude in your heart. Thankfulness is not necessary as gratitude alone is the feeling of being thankful.

It will be the elements themselves that make the change in order for you to 'see'. Now, close your eyes, start the chant and I will guide you on our walk but do not open your eyes until I tell you."

"Right, got it," I replied rolling my eyes as I closed them.

So off we went, walking through the downtown core of the city amongst oil executives, lawyers, engineers and doctors with me chanting some silly Sumerian diddy and a tall foreign looking guy holding onto my arm. It must have been a sight for sore eyes.

This went on for about 15 to 20 minutes which at the time seemed like an eternity then finally Enki said those fateful words, 'OK, open your eyes now'.

I opened my eyes and froze in my tracks. The world was gone and in its place was swirling smoke and whipped cream all intertwined with neon colours. The colours were changing in brightness and intensity like the northern lights on a clear cold evening in northern Alberta.

 While the wispy clouds were dancing and changing colours, shapes were phasing in and out of my range of visibility. Small strands of piano wires were snaking back and forth like someone snapping a whip or like school girls skipping the double rope.

Nothing was solid anymore. Even the concrete and steel floor that we were standing on 15 feet above the street looked like a very fine grid of small wires that had been illuminated with neon colours. Strangely enough, the wires were transparent as I could clearly see the street below. I had never seen concrete and rebar look so fluffy.

Strangest of all were the odd, egg-shaped luminescent blobs that kept bouncing past me. They were layer upon layer of luminescence that was both transparent and semi-transparent which constantly changed colours seemingly from the inside out. It occurred to me that the blobs were people since there were a lot of them and they were moving in a fashion that would suggest they were going somewhere.

 Some blobs were larger than others, some were brightly coloured while others were dull. All of them were basically the same shape but it was how they moved that captured my attention. It was like someone in a potato sack race trying to bounce their way across the finish line only the sack seemed weightless and was not touching the ground.

I took a more concentrated look at my surroundings. What used to be solid objects like walls and furniture were now wavy lines of luminescent spaghetti. It seemed that I could put my hand through a solid object if I wanted and so I gave it a try. The solid wall that was straight away in front of me gave way in a swirl of vapour as the luminescent spaghetti parted and my hand passed through unobstructed with but a slight tingle as small sparks flew from my fingertips.

I sensed that someone was trying to communicate with me but instead of hearing it in my ears, I literally could see the sound waves swirling towards me, bending around me and washing up against me. Somehow my brain was interpreting the sound as a coloured wave pulsing towards me and when it hit, it was like an ocean wave, splashing and bending around a pier. As it splashed past I was able to see a rainbow of colour ebbing and flowing just like after a heavy rain. Each colour and each pulse was being interpreted in my brain in a different and unusual way. Instead of recognizing the sounds as separate words and sentences, I was only grasping the idea or the concept of the coloured wave form.

I could tell that Enki was talking to me but instead of hearing his voice as discreet words like, "OK – Jim – I – now – want – you – to – direct – a – thought – at – a blob – of – your – choice. It was more like OKJimInowwantyoutodirectathougtatablobofyourcoice. One concept directed at me in the form of an undulating wave of spectacularly brilliant colours.

It was not hard to grasp what he was saying since it was what I would interpret as a more natural form of communicating. It seemed to take no effort whatsoever to unravel the packet of information but it was tremendously distracting having an ocean wave pour over my head spilling glorious colours in its wake.

In fact, I was so distracted that Enki repeated his command in a more forceful way to grab my attention. This resulted in a bigger wave splashing more brilliant colours around and I started to laugh. My laughing caused an even more spectacular event with every colour of the rainbow exploding outwards from my position bouncing off of every energy surface that was within sight, if you could call it that. They mixed, merged and intermingled with the grid of energy fields. Eventually, I came around to my demented senses and replied to Enki by simply thinking my reply then watched as the thought wave emanate from my body and flowed outward in a cacophony of colours. "What do you mean."

Enki seemed to understand and sent a color pulse back to me that I interpreted as, "Quit being a dumb shit and listen to what I am saying. Pick a blob and direct a thought towards it and watch the color, shape and texture of the blob. Let's start with a disparaging thought such as, you are the ugliest piece of crap I have ever seen, and I would like nothing better than to punch you in your stupid looking face."

I grasped the idea/concept as it came across as a very visually dark coloured wave with a rather nasty looking peak. Being the dutiful student I was, I looked out across the energy grid or what a normal person would call a floor and picked a blob bouncing past at random and sent out the thought packet as instructed.

I then observed the blob with my new found senses which seemed to kick into hypersensitive mode.

The thought wave went out not so much like a pebble dropped in a pond of calm water but more like I had blown a big cloud of smoke toward the blob and indeed the color of the thought form was dark grey and black, intermixed.

 It engulfed the blob then dissipated but the effect was not to be missed. The smoke seemed to cause a dent or a large concave dish in the side of the blob. Then the transparency of the blob dimmed and became more opaque with a dark patch emerging on the side where the nasty smoke idea had first impacted. Finally, there was a visible hardening of the outer shell of the blob like it had formed a second protective skin or layer. The blob however did not shift its orientation nor slow down or speed up its gait. It just kept hopping along like nothing had happened. Everything that I saw was stored away in packets, not inside my head but somewhere outside of my body. At that point I realized that I too must be a blob.

Then from somewhere behind me and engulfing me like a cloud of billowing colours another thought form came from Enki. "Now, pick another blob at random and formulate a different thought packet such as expressing love, companionship and acceptance like you would desire to be this blobs friend. Do it now".

Being the decent chap that I was, I targeted a blob and sent the thought form out quick as a whistle.

This time however the smoke that I was blowing was a different color, much brighter and more compelling. When the smoke hit, the blob reacted in quite the opposite way as it immediately brightened and the outer skin seemed to become thinner. The blob's bright glittery inside seemed to glow and looked like it was now closer to the surface.

I thought that this was quite remarkable and even though this thought was supposed to stay inside my head, it went out as a coloured wave-form just like all the others. The realization that struck me was that my thoughts were no longer hidden inside my head. They were not just available to me but were also available to whoever could interpret and "see" the coloured waveforms.

I was standing there thinking these thoughts and seeing them emanate outwards from my body but I could not sense my body as being a part of me. I could sense that it was there, I just couldn't see it.

At first I thought I was a blob as well but realized as I tried to look down at my feet and hold my hands out in front of my eyes that there were no blobbish appendages. It was then that I realized that I was not using my eyes to see the colours, waveforms, blobs and energy grid.

 For the life of me I couldn't figure out what I was using to see all of this amazing stuff as I could have been looking out the end of my dick for all I knew.

I was deep in contemplation on my visual sensory perception when I felt a sharp crack across the back of my shoulders. It was at that precise moment that it occurred to me that my eyes had been closed. I opened them and behold, the world was back to normal. I turned to see Enki with a big shit-grin on his face, eyes bright with a look of sheer delight.

"So," he began, "One thing that I would like you to take away from this little experience of ours is that what you saw was more realistic in terms of what the universe is like, than what you are seeing now. Do you understand what I am saying?"

"Yeah, sure," I replied. "The world is made up of people who are blobs, thoughts that are coloured tsunamis, concrete that is pulsing energy grid-lines and walls made out of neon spaghetti. I haven't got a clue as to what you are talking about Enki."

"Let's start with thoughts then. As you saw, thoughts are real and have an effect on those around you. Your brain is like a microwave tower that emits signals all the time. You brain waves however, are more complex. A portion of these waves can be measured and you call them alpha and beta waves. There is another portion than cannot be measured.

Think of radio waves. They are emitted by a beacon and travel through the air as an electromagnetic wave. When the wave is picked up by an electronic device it broadcasts a sound that your auditory nerve interprets as music.

However, there is no device that can pick-up the frequencies emitted by the human brain that pertain to thought. The frequencies that can be measured only give your scientists a vague indication of the various activity states of the brain.

The brain frequency that is associated with though exists as a completely different wave form that transmits from your head and impacts those around you, as you saw.

No one can read your thoughts, they are your own. But everyone feels what you are thinking even if they don't immediately sense it or realize it. Do you remember when I asked you to think a disparaging thought and direct it towards a random person passing by?"

"Yes, the person changed color and a dent appeared in his/her side which quickly disappeared."

"Correct, you saw the effect. It was real and even though on a conscious level, that person never gave it another thought, she felt something inside that she couldn't explain. Suddenly she became sad for no seemingly apparent reason.

That random person was a woman by the way, even though you could not tell. When you are more practiced you will be able to see that the outer protective layer is thicker with men that it is with women.

Women are more able to sense the thoughts of those around them even though they cannot interpret them."

"That explains a lot about women," I said.

"Some, who you would describe as psychic, have come much closer to reading the thoughts of those around them. Psychics are mostly women because of this innate sensing ability. Women also pay more attention to their feelings than men."

"That's right," I said. "For men to get in touch with their feelings with regards to other men, they have to punch each other in the face."

"Right you are," replied Enki. "But thoughts are much more than passing gusts of wind that put small dents in the protective coating of people. Thoughts go out and collect energy. They collect these energy units and use them as building blocks."

"What in god's name are you talking about Enki? Energy units, building blocks?

"Just as bricks are laid one upon the other with cement to hold them together, energy units come together in a similar fashion as well. It is the collection and coalescence of energy units as directed by intelligent thought that has guided the construction of the world around you.

Nothing in this world is built without the energy of thought behind it. A few minutes ago when you were "seeing" for the first time, the solid world that you knew became the real world of energy. I induced this new sense into your mental capacity temporarily with the help of the first density elements.

The energy grid is always there in its infinite colors and wavelength. But in your normal state, when you open your eyes to see the world that you live in, the energy grid collapses into solid form. Not in absolute reality but only in your mind. You see, the energy signature travels along the optic nerve as an electro magnetic pulse. The brain interprets these pulses and forms the visual image of a brick wall, say.

Your other senses faithfully agree with the interpretation such that your hand against the brick wall feels its sturdiness and impresses upon the mind its structural existence. A few moments ago, if you remember, you passed your hand through a wall. This was accomplished by my ability to short-circuit your normal senses and have you interpret your reality in a different way. The wall was still a wall. Nothing about the physical existence of the wall, as a solid object or a wave form had changed. Only your interpretation of the wall changed."

"Yes, but Enki, there were other people there. Surly someone saw me put my hand through that wall?"

"There were other people who saw you to be sure. What they saw however was your hand resting against the surface of the wall. The electro-magnetic impulse that carried the image of your hand resting inside the wall was filtered by their brain and replaced with an image that made more sense. It was your hand resting on the wall that kept the world normal for the people who saw you. The brain and its ability to keep things in check is very powerful.

What I have tried to show you is the nature of your reality and how you exist within it. It is a construct initiated by the sub-logos which is supported and propped up by the inner workings of each and every individual who is on the face of the earth today. Every one of you are co-creators in this reality, which is really an illusion, based on how you collectively want it to be in order to provide the stimulus or catalyst for growth.

Again, growth is achieved by creating situations and events that are challenging and hard work. Picture getting fired from your job, losing your best friend in a bush fire, having your wife run off with the guy next door or finding out all your kids are on methamphetamines.

No worry, it's an illusion. What makes the whole thing more challenging for you is that you haven't the slightest idea that it is a game. A game that you play on yourself. But then it has to be that way so that you and the rest of your fellow humans do the proper work.

So put the dead to rest with remorse or compassion, forgive your boss or curse him, kick your wife's ass in divorce court or welcome her back and get your kids help or abandon them. See what I mean? You can act in a positive way or in a negative way. It is your choice.

Then when the time is right you will understand that the game is just a game and you are in the final 2 minutes. The game will be over soon then it's harvest time and that is why I am here, to help with the harvest."

"So, are you a farmer now?" I quipped

"Yes, in a way, you might call me that," he replied. "I have come to help those that are ready."

"OK, so this is getting a bit weird. You are saying that some will graduate while others will fail?"

"Not quite, as fail is the wrong word, although you are close. Those who graduate will stay and transition into fourth density where they will begin a new era of work, growth and learning.

Those who do not graduate will leave, it is true, but this is because they are not ready for forth density work as more time is required in third. It takes a certain level of spiritual development and darn hard work to qualify. Like the Marines. They will go to a new place to carry on third density work until someday they too are ready."

"Where is this new place?"

"I don't know as this information was not important to my mission. I only know that it is being prepared as we speak."

"OK, fair enough, but what does fourth density work entail and how do you know if you are ready to graduate?"

"Fourth density work is that of love. Love is an infinite concept and a powerful force in the universe. To understand and utilize the power of love takes many millions of your earth years to master and it must be studied under vastly different conditions than those found on earth here today.

Love is a massively powerful concept or force in the universe. Love is not just a special feeling that you might have for another person but think of it as an energy that the very universe was built upon. It permeates everything and is responsible for every known power source and law in the entire universes. All of it is built upon love even though humans may look around and not get a sense of this at all.

So literally millions of years are spent discovering all the truths of love and this is what 4th density work is all about.

But when the transition takes place a very interesting phenomenon will happen on earth. The 3rd dimension is based upon the 3rd chakra which is associated with will. The corresponding wavelength or color of this dimension is yellow. The sun reflects this dimension and shines as a yellow orb. When the earth and all those on it transition to 4th density the sun will shine green to reflect a new emphasis on the heart chakra which of course represents love. Green is the color of love.

Third density work entails awareness, consciousness and experience of the mind/body/soul complex in a pressure cooker world. Catalyst provides the experiences by which you develop and become aware. Catalyst could possibly be defined as every challenging, joyful, frightful, wonderful, horrible and debilitating experience that comes your way while in 3rd density bodies.

Development continues until there is sufficient evidence that an entity has taken a definitive step along the positive or negative path. There are 25,000 year cycles with three such cycles being the allotted time for entities to progress based on the multitude of incarnations that they have experienced.

Then you embark upon the next journey as defined by the path you have chosen. For some, you will have started down one path then realized that it was not the one you were comfortable with. It did not resonate with your inner being and so the steps are retracted.

For others the path chosen is well defined and travelled with vigour, be it positive or negative. Most will not see the path at all or it will be ill-defined and poorly lit. This usually leads to confusion and a great fuzzy middle ground which is chosen by default. This middle ground leads nowhere and essentially means the mind/body/spirit entity is not ready for advancement. That is why 3rd density will have to be repeated over and over again until there is a realization that we are on a journey and that the journey requires advancement.

The game played here is complicated. You die and remember who you are then you are born and forget it all. This is trial by fire and everyone agrees to the conditions otherwise it would not be so. Life in the 3rd dimension is all about experience, my friend, hard gut wrenching experience.

Now to answer your last question, how do you know if you are ready for work in 4th density? Well you don't. Say you are always thinking of yourself before anyone or anything else, you are probably ready for fourth density negative work. Likewise, if you mostly think about others before you think of yourself or put others before yourself, then more than likely, you are ready for 4th density positive work. But I will talk more about his later.

This is quite enough for your little pea brain to absorb, today."

Chapter 5: Mind/Body/Spirit

I went to bed that night and had crazy, vivid dreams that haunted me the next morning. In my dream I was walking through a field all alone when suddenly a group of thugs appeared who looked like they wanted to mug me or worse. I became frightened and wanted desperately to get away but I was essentially surrounded. It then occurred to me that I could fly and so I lifted off the ground and soared away from the sorry lot whose intention was to shuck me like an oyster. Being shucked was something I had never experienced before and I didn't want to find out now.

Much to my dismay however there were several fellows who appeared to have the same ability to fly and lifted off to chase after me. Fortunately, I was able to out fly them and got away unscathed. I woke up in a cold sweat and thanked the good lord that the dream had ended.

The dream's meaning, upon further reflection, seemed to say that I was surrounded by limiting ideas about life. Those ideas try to trap me and hold me down but realizing who I am and what I am doing here sets me free. That's not to say there will be those that chase me down despite this realization.

I also had this crazy dream that I flew to Mars with Enki but that was just a little too crazy even for me.

It was Saturday morning and so my wife and I, as per our usual routine got up and set out for coffee at our favourite little shop down about half a block from our apartment. It was a nice sunny morning and the coffee tasted especially good when I broached the subject of my recent encounter with Enki.

I had given my wife the reader's digest version of the previous sessions with my new friend but now I wanted to share the full brunt of yesterday's experience more as a sanity check than a friendly exchange.

"You won't believe the conversation I had with Enki yesterday," I began. "I saw him at the Coffee Shop after you left for work and we had a brilliant conversation which lasted most of the morning. He was telling me all sorts of weird stuff and then I saw something that I have never seen before. I am going to tell you what I saw and you have to tell me if you think that I have turned into a nut bar, you know, a whack job."

"OK," she said. "But can I answer the question before you tell me the story?"

"Oh, good one," I replied.

I told her the whole story about how Enki had turned the world into an energy grid with neon lights and coloured smoke, not leaving out a single thing, not even the dumb-ass chant which left me feeling like a dipstick.

"So what this has done," I went on to say, "is to give me a new perspective about who we are, what we are doing here and the reality of the world in which we live in."

"I see," she replied. "Now that you have this big idea about life, and you have had a strange hallucinatory experience, how does it all fit? I mean with your own experiences and all."

"Well," I replied. "This is the thing. We aren't who we think we are according to Enki. We are something much bigger and much more fantastic. We are mind/body/spirit entities and each segment is composed of sub- parts. Now don't forget, this is Enki doing the talking and me doing the listening. I am not saying I buy it, well maybe parts of it, but there is still a lot of figuring out to do before I go preaching in the city streets."

"Didn't you say you went walking around downtown chanting some ancient Sumerian phrase?"

"Yes, well that's not preaching, you know. In most cases it's called, 'losing a bet' but this is really weird and if I can explain it to you and it makes any kind of sense, then that becomes a bit of a reality check for me. Plus, it helps to have it straight in my head if I can get it straight in yours."

"Good, now start me at the beginning and tell me about how this all fits together in our apparent make-up."

"OK, Enki insists that we have three parts, mind, body and soul which is nothing earth shattering since most folk know this part already. But there is more to it than meets the eye."

I started to talk and then something very strange happened. While I was talking, the words seemed to be coming from somewhere else. The sounds and utterances of speech were coming from my mouth but the content was coming from god-knows-where. I realized what I was saying had not come from Enki since he had not uttered a single word about what I was droning on about. The words were being heard by my wife and me for the first time.

I went on to say, "When we look at the mind for example, we have to consider various parts or sub-compartments. There is the outer ego which is the part of us that we identify with most. This is the part that you see when you look in the mirror. That same part that looks out from behind your eyes and interprets the world according to what it sees, hears, smells, feels and touches.

When we are consciously aware of ourselves, it is the ego that is aware. The ego has a very important task in that he/she must navigate this world and experience all the things that happen in our lives and interpret them as best it can to make sense of things.

Mostly however, we are taught at an early age by our parents about how things work and what to believe. We are also taught at a young age what not to believe such as imaginary friends, fairies, dragons and the like. Then later we are taught that either god is in control, if our parents are religious or chance and fate are at work if they are atheists. Therefore, we see the world through the eyes of our parents until we are old enough to think for ourselves and have experiences that would either support or deny the belief. This is the work of the ego.

When we come of age we will have had enough experiences of our own to find the answers for ourselves. In Tarot this is called the Fool's Journey not because it's foolish to embark upon the journey but because it is taken with almost no thought or planning or as some might call, 'reckless abandon' if you will."

"Yes, I see that and understand it, but where does the funky part come in. So far everything you have said is quite ordinary. I am dying to hear the good stuff."

"Splendid, so let's get on to the next part which is called the inner self. This is still part of the mind and is sometimes called the sub-conscious and has been given a bum rap over the last century or so.

Carl Jung spent a lot of time focussed on the sub-conscious as did Sigmund Freud. The only problem was, these guys demonized the sub-conscious. They postulated that all of the nasty things that we think of, like killing the neighbour's dog because it barks all night, swirls around in our mind and comes from the sub-conscious."

"Swirls around in your mind you mean."

"I assume other guys have that kind of junk swirling around too, I don't know. Anyway where was I? Oh yeah, the sub-conscious as portrayed by our modern science is a portion of our psyche hidden deep inside us that drives us towards certain things. A machination of the physical brain.

Sometimes demented dreams, desires and morbid thoughts are referred to as the demon within. However, when your inner self is looked upon as the real you, then you start to understand a very important part of yourself. The inner self is not part of the organic body.

This part is the immortal part of who we really are. The part that is never destroyed or goes away. The part that continues to grow, evolve and develop throughout eternity. We are not swallowed into the void of nothingness when we die but continue on in our true form, that of the inner self. A conscious spirit/entity personality.

So if we consider for a moment that we are immortal beings and we transition from life to life in the never-ending pursuit of development and value fulfilment, then our inner self takes on new meaning. We are a compilation of many lives, many personalities and many experiences which all become part of your immortal self or inner self. It's what we might call, the real you.

You are continually 'growing' and it is the inner self that gathers these personalities and experiences and absorbs them so that you are continually becoming everything that you have ever been.

Each life we live, we learn and grow and that all gets captured by and incorporated into your inner self so that not even a single memory of the smallest event in the multitude of existences ever gets lost.

Even though in your present life you may not remember a spring day in 1567 when you were a young man going off to war, or sitting for the first time with the elders of the tribe discussing the next buffalo hunt, those memories are available to you at your beckoning call. They will be as vivid as the day you experienced them when you transition back to your real self.

A scent, a first kiss, a feeling or melody no matter how far back in time is remembered intimately like it had happened just a moment ago and forever retained by the inner self. In fact, when you die, you then become your real self. The inner self.

The outer ego is temporary, limited and allows you to function in the world at a particular time. The inner self, the real you, is forever and retains everything that you have ever done."

"Whew, that is a lot of information," my wife interceded. "I can see why you come home looking like someone has beaten you over the head with a baseball bat. But how can we be sure of any of this stuff. I know I can look in the mirror and see myself there. I know that I can look out at the world and see buildings and streets and houses and cars. If I can see, hear, smell and touch something, then that makes it real for me.

But I can't do that with my inner self, at least, I don't think I can since this is the first I have heard of such a thing. Why doesn't my inner self step out in front and say hi, I'm the big you, how do you do."

"Life would be a lot easier if we knew there was a superman inside us with magical powers that could help us get out of tough situations, I agree. But then Enki said it wasn't supposed to be easy and that life is full of trials and tribulations for good reason. But the inner self is ready and willing to help, we just need to ask and then make an attempt to get to know him/her which of course is I/you.

Apparently meditation and visualisation are the answers to connecting with your inner self. It's like visualizing getting together with a close friend in an exquisite place; say a beach or at a lake in the woods or on a mountaintop. I suppose it's just like anything else where it takes an effort to meet people in a new town for example. When you begin the visualizations and meditations and they are performed with genuine care then the connection begins to take place. Now you have a very powerful guide to help with life events.

There is also this convenient concept called 'the veil' which suggests all is hidden from us, while we play the game called life and that is probably why it is difficult to connect with our inner self. Many of us don't believe there is such a thing because it is so effectively hidden.

When we are born, the veil is drawn and we go into a forgetting mode which gives us the chance, I suppose, to play the game of life for real. Enki said that we would not learn the lessons needed if we knew the game was a fake. It would be a waste of time for all of us.

I guess that might be considered a major cop-out to explain the unexplainable, but don't you think that whatever theory we are asked to believe or whatever religion we are a part of, all contain this element of faith.

Faith is involved in everything we think and do as it always comes down to the lack of definitive proof that a thing happened or could happen. Do we really know if Achilles was the greatest warrior ever or an elaborate myth? Does the story become a myth because his father was a god and his mother a mortal? Sounds familiar to me when I think of the other guy whose father was a god, and mother was a virgin.

 When it comes right down to it, it doesn't really matter. Look at the theory of evolution as a modern day example. Our scientists would have you believe that we somehow evolved from a single-celled amoeba in the primordial soup 6 billion years ago. What nonsense and Enki says it didn't happen that way at all so who am I supposed to believe, scientists who are supposedly smart but support a dumb theory, or some wacko I met in a bar in Vietnam.

Then Judaism would have us believe that some god created a fellow named Adam 6000 years ago and then extracted a rib from his body to create his main squeeze, Eve. I must say, however, I like Enki's story better, it's more plausible but there isn't a hope in hell of proving any of it.

The Catholic Church would have us believe that the dude whose mother was a virgin came to forgive our sins and save us so that we can have everlasting life. We already have life everlasting if you believe Enki, and furthermore, what sins have I committed and what am I being saved from?

It has always bothered me that some guy ate an apple 6000 years ago and somehow I am guilty by association. The church calls it original sin and now I am going off to hell unless I am saved?

This has always been the part I can't wrap my head around. Why did God create a situation in which he knew we would fail then condemn us for failing unless we bought into a solution that only he could provide? But I digress.

The second part revolves around the body. Now the body is easy to understand as we can look in the mirror, see our bodies and feel them. Plus when something happens that causes hurt or trauma, we feel pain. So the body is easiest to sense and explain. However, it doesn't stop there as our bodies also possess a consciousness that goes beyond our understanding.

Our body is conscious and is separate from what we think it is. We tend to think of our body as something we ride around in like a car and when some parts wear out we replace them. When some function is impaired we repair it. We think we sense the world around us and feel things through our bodies but this is not true. The body receives signals from the environment which are then interpreted or translated by the mind. But the body feels other things as well, things beyond the normal functioning of our senses. We tend to ignore those signals and messages because they do not conform to what we have been taught.

As a child, our experiences were pure and the body told us many things that we took to be true. Then as we got older, we were told those odd shapes we saw in the shadows, the little voices we heard or those special invisible friends that we saw were not real. We were taught to disregard those things as an overly active imagination, not as perfectly reliable stimuli being faithfully transmitted to you by your body. Heaven forbid that we should hear the thoughts of animals in the forest or the whisper of trees. We have effectively learned to shut off our bodies.

And so we let a doctor tell us that we are sick when we already know it. However, going to a doctor means that he can put a name to our ailments and prescribe pills to cover off the symptoms.

What if your body not only told you that something was wrong but was willing and able to correct the issue with some prompting and encouragement from you, its best friend? With this kind of union and understanding, you have a very powerful combination of health and vitality brought on by a loving relationship between you and your body.

Scientists know that it takes literally millions of electrical impulses to produce muscle contractions, tendon manipulation and nerve endings firing to complete a single movement of our hand or foot. We do not think, OK foot move 1.03ft forward while you, the other foot wait for 2.6 seconds and then move ahead 2.64ft and thus complete one step. We just move and take it for granted that the step will be completed without stumbling or falling. The body takes care of this without the mind having to think about it as a free gesture of love and willingness to function as it was meant to.

That might mean the body and mind have separate consciousnesses but the design of this system was meant to work closely together as one. The medical profession does not recognize the body as a consciousness unto its own and insists it is the involuntary system which does the work. A system that sits in behind our awareness and does its own thing. To a certain extent this is true but what doctors fail to understand is that you can link up with the body consciousness and gleam what has gone wrong and fix it. Kind of like a faithful old pick-up truck.

This may seem trivial but the body interacts with the mind at a level that we do not fathom. Disease, for example, is the body's faithful replication of the machinations of the mind. With some, the mind knowingly communicates with the body and the body responds to the requests in like fashion. This is the same as setting up communication with the inner self, it requires practice and visualizations.

Nothing is easy or automatic but getting to know the body consciousness is a worthwhile endeavor. In fact, Enki says the three parts of you should all be aware of each other and work in unison. It seems that the two underneath parts, the inner self and body self are aware of the ego but the ego is completely unaware of them. This applies to most people but of course there are those special folk who realize there is more than meets the eye."

"So how does this work then?" asked my wife. "If we are made up of these different parts and maybe god doesn't exist or evolution didn't happen then what are we supposed to believe? How does it all work?"

"I was hoping we would get to that because it is what every person everywhere in the world should eventually ask themselves once there is the realization that the current smorgasbord of beliefs available to us are all fatally flawed," I replied.

"First of all, Yahweh, the Jewish war god of the Old Testament and Enki's All That Is or as he sometimes says The One Infinite Creator are two completely different concepts.

Enki says the Jewish God Yahweh was originally a synthesis that came about from Abraham trying to understand the gods' dealing with men. In particular Enlil and Enki were the two main Sumerian gods whom intervened in human lives and this was Abraham's way of making sense of it all.

Every nation at that time had a god and they were all various forms of the original Sumerian gods. Enki and his family formed a portion of the pantheon of gods while Enlil and his kin formed the others. Between the two brothers and their families, the Sumerians, Egyptians, Hitites, Canaanites, Israelites, Babylonians, Assyrians, Aztecs and Incas all paid homage to Enlil and Enki and various members of their families in one form or another.

The One Infinite Creator, however, is an all-encompassing creative force that exists in and through its creation. We are all part of All That Is therefore we too are creative beings. Enlil and Enki know this better than anyone.

 We create our world, ourselves, our circumstances in life and everything else for that matter. The world exists by virtue of our thoughts and it is the thoughts of every single person on the face of the earth that prop up our world.

The things that we see such as a concrete building or brick walls exist only because we choose that they exist. They exist because we collectively think them into existence. Sure the concrete is made at a cement factory and delivered to the work site and the building goes up stage by stage. Instant manifestation is not a part of our reality such that thinking of a building causes it to appear.

But we hold the building first as a concept in our minds before the actual construction starts. It takes shape in our minds then we go out and get money, an architect, sub-contractors and put together a plan. One year later, maybe two the building is standing before us in its magnificence. It didn't go poof but it is there just the same; a product of our imagination and wilful intent.

 It is not our ego that is at work here, it is our inner self. It is this portion of every living person on earth that holds buildings up.

Otherwise they are just spaghetti noodles of neon energy strings. The inner self works continually in association with other selves to bring about the circumstances and events that happen globally, culturally and personally.

Enki says that buildings are held up by thought, not bricks and mortar.

It is just like the background workings of our body consciousness that allow us to take a simple step forward. The inner self collaborates with others to bring about a spring day or a nasty storm as they meet the needs of the collective people involved. Nothing happens by accident or chance and nothing goes on without some degree of planning that happens at another level. Crazy eh."

"So if what you are saying is reasonably true," my wife went on to say. "It would seem to me, then, that if a group of people pointed at a red rose and said it was red, while a single person came along and said it was yellow, there would exist a disagreement.

Quite simply, the yellow rose person would be wrong by virtue of a so-called collective reality. The yellow rose person may be color blind or argumentative but ultimately the universe is in check.

But let's say that 5 guys walk up to a brick wall and punch it, you would expect 5 guys to walk away with broken and bloodied knuckles. All is good until a 6th guy comes along and throws a punch at the wall and has his hand pass through and back out, completely unscathed. Now what?"

"Well", I replied. "We have a problem. If the guy whose hand passed through the wall was able to reproduce the effect over and over again, under severe scientific scrutiny, then I suppose we would have to say this one person had special powers.

However, if this person was able to teach others the technique used to punch a brick wall unscathed such that anyone now could punch brick walls as if they were shadow boxing, then we would have to rewrite the books on physics and we would have to rethink the world around us.

But if things need to change such that an odd occurrence as the one described is needed to usher in a new paradigm or era (whatever that might be), then that decision is made at an inner level and all are involved.

Do you think electricity was discovered just in the last 200 years? Were there not people who flew kites in electrical storms 2000 years ago, or perhaps ol' Alex just got lucky and wasn't electrocuted. Maybe he dreamt about dancing with electrons and had an idea that he had been contemplating for years and years before getting the guts to fly his kite.

It seems that all great discoveries are made when someone does something by accident. It may be considered that all great discoveries in the last 200 years are just re-discoveries as there is evidence that ancient civilizations may have been as advanced or more advanced than ours.

Did the Sumerians have electricity? I'll have to ask Enki that one. Did they have flying machines? Enki certainly says they did, but who knows. There is no proof. It opens the door to other crazy phenomena that only requires some thought and imagination to reorder our world. Can you imagine if someone figured out how to fly without the use of a machine of any type using some odd chant?"

"You ought to know how to do that."

"Yes, well let's say someone figured out how to travel from point A to B without gasoline, electricity, jet fuel or any other form of energy. Then let's say he could teach that ability to whomever and for a mere $1.00 you too could learn to fly to work or take your family on a holiday without getting in a car or airplane. Wouldn't that turn the world upside down?

The guys from Exxon, Shell and Ford would go broke as nobody would need to buy their products anymore.

I've had many dreams about flying and in those dreams I would close my eyes, think about lifting off the ground and then I would get light-headed. Upon opening my eyes, I would begin to lift off the ground and start my journey upwards. It always worked and was always exhilarating."

We went about the rest of the morning bantering back and forth about all sorts of crazy things that could happen if it was as easy as intent being the basis of our reality. Or even if our thoughts immediately manifested and what that would look like.

Apparently, this was what the ancient Egyptian mystery schools were all about. They were trying to teach students how to control their thoughts such that when they developed the ability to manifest at will, they didn't conjure up crazy things like fire-breathing dragons and blood hungry raptors. I had to remember to ask Enki to give me the skinny on ancient Egypt because apparently he was there."

"What about the spirit," my wife asked. "You said that there were 3 parts and the third part was the spirit."

"Spirit is the part that I have the most trouble with," I replied. "It's not that the spirit is a concept that is hard to understand, it's the part about being a hologram of All That Is and the thing about being immortal that causes my brain to feel like it has been baked.

I guess it's easy to understand that as humans we have a beginning and an end but as spirit there is neither. A concept we attribute to God but not to ourselves. I understand that we come from spirit but where did the spirit come from?

Somehow the spirit is linked to, or a part of, All That Is, but there is also this thing about coming from darkness into the light. We always associate the darkness with foreboding or evil so this seems to go against the origin of spirit or All That Is.

I often wonder how much of our human nature comes from the spirit. Or how much of our true authentic spirit-nature do we carry with us into this realm of experience."

"Well, I guess that answers a lot about why your brain is incapacitated," replied my wife.

CHAPTER 6: REQUIREMENTS FOR FOURTH DENSITY

I met up again with Enki several days later and had more questions than answers. As per usual we met at our familiar coffee shop and embarked upon the continuation of our conversation from last time.

"OK," I started. "Let's pick up where we left off by telling me more about how a person qualifies for 4th density work."

"That's a good place to get started," Enki replied. "Qualifying for 4th density work requires making a choice in 3rd density. But to qualify for the harvest, one must be steadfast in the choice and it must be clearly made. However, most do not know they are in a choosing situation to begin with, because of the veil. If one were to know for example that a certain percentage of intent was required to make the transition to 4th density, then probably it would be easier to attain. That is, if one actually wished to attain the level."

"Right, then the obvious question would be, what the hell does that mean?"

"What I am trying to say is that if you desire to attain 4th density via a positively polarized route, then it will take a certain level of intent. If, however you desire to attain 4th density via the negative route, it then requires a more focused intent."

"Wait a minute, you mean that it requires more effort to be negatively polarized?"

"Yes, that is correct and the reason for that comes from the Creator himself as it was determined early on that it was better for most mind/body/spirit complexes to seek the creator via the positive path. Since free will is at work during this cycle, both paths were made available but obviously one was given preference. So All That Is in her infinite wisdom made the preferable path easier to follow than the less desirable path but ultimately, each is equally valid and each lead back to her. One emphasizes love while the other focuses on power."

"So how was one path made easier and the other harder? How does this work?"

"It works by virtue of intent. If you have made the choice to take the negative route, your focus on serving self must be 95% or greater. You must think mostly of how to manipulate and dominate others to the exclusive benefit of self. All of your actions, thoughts, desires, conversations and doings must exhibit a 95% or better desire to serve self.

So you see, there is a high level of dedication required to do this work. It does not require a person to be evil or cruel as there is really no such thing as evil except as the antithesis of good. The concept of good and evil was introduced many millennia ago as a way to distract humans and distort events. In the spirit world which represents infinity, good and evil do not exist.

There are many people today that move in a negatively polarized direction. People who work at high levels in government and industry all desire to have many beneath them ready and willing to do their bidding. The rich and powerful are mostly all negatively polarized to an extent greater than 50%.

This was what Jesus was trying to say when he talked about the difficulty of a rich man entering the kingdom of heaven. He was actually saying that it is difficult for a rich man to choose a positively polarized path but the editors of the bible wanted to create the concept of heaven and hell and so they changed the words. Rich and powerful equates to negative polarization but as always there are exceptions.

Many times even the middle man on the totem pole can become negatively polarized if he dominates those below him as wilfully and energetically as those above do to him.

The hierarchical structure that is representative of a negatively polarized civilization is almost always put in place with the use of violence. It is the only way a negative social structure can turn chaos into order. You see, a negative society will turn upon each other and continue to war and kill each other until either all are dead or a hierarchy is established by the ordering of groups, factions and individuals.

The most powerful individuals advance to the top by plundering, pillaging, lying and killing while placing trusted associates below to protect the regime and their own selfish interests. Rival regimes will continue to fight until all are disposed and there is only one left. Once this happens the ordering begins with those loyal to the new master being placed in positions of importance but always below, while those disloyal during the period of chaos are exterminated or placed in the lowest of low positions to serve all the masters above.

For a person to become harvestable on the positive side, the intent need only be 55%. So you see that it is easier to follow the path of love, acceptance and forgiveness in an effort to serve others."

"But if you have to be better than 55% to graduate under the positive banner or greater than 95% to be eligible for 4th density negative work, does that not mean there are quite a few that fall in the preverbal gap. That in-between spot that could be called ignorance or even apathy," I replied.

"My, aren't we perceptive today. That is exactly right. There is a wide spot in the road called indifference and that is where most wind up. That is why it takes multiple cycles of 75,000 years for the majority of mind/body/spirit complexes to graduate.

Now, you may also realize that the veil has two purposes. The first is to make the game that you play more real and second is to hide the reason for being here in the first place. If you knew early in your evolution that a choice was required and the parameters of the choice were given, you would complete 3rd density quickly before all the lessons were learned. Or you may construct many pleasurable lives and not progress at all.

Therefore, the intent that I had talked about earlier must come from somewhere authentic. Your natural inclinations come into play here to establish your direction of intent. Then over the multiple lives that you lead, the path develops. That is not to say that you cannot change your path or direction mid-stride since there is always free will at play.

There is such a diversity of life experiences on this earth plane with kings and queens enjoying riches, prestige and power on one end while paupers, beggars and thieves live on the other. Even now, the richness of experience is more widespread than ever. You can start out life as a ghetto hoodlum, get discovered at a talent show and go on to enjoy riches and fame. A young boy grows up in the back of a van because his dad can't get a decent paying job and then goes on to fame and fortune in the movie industry vowing never to be like his dad.

Rich people lose it all and become poor while poor people get rich and all the while very few understand what it is all about. Information was given to humans throughout history to help you along since it is a difficult task but unfortunately you are all quite dumb.

Rich doesn't matter, poor doesn't matter and power doesn't matter. What matters is how rich or poor makes you feel. Whether you choose to swim in an ocean of wealth or tread water in a pool of poverty is immaterial. Death strikes, and takes the rich as vigorously and energetically as the poor. Once out of body, the entity realizes that it didn't matter. What mattered was the experience and experience doesn't necessarily equate to fame and fortune."

"I hope Brad Pitt figures this out before he dies," I quipped.

 "Many important figures have come to deliver the message that you are immortal," replied Enki. "They have come to this earth plane to tell you that to experience life as fully as possible is what's important. No matter what your position is in life. Some even hinted at the choice but usually in very obscure terms. Your Brad Pitt is a young soul as the term is used. He has come to this world only recently and has chosen fame and fortune to start with. He will no doubt go on to experience pain and suffering in other lives to balance out this one.

There were a few advanced souls who came to deliver important message to mankind. A fellow named Buddha tried to tell you, then Krishna and finally a dude named Jesus took a stab.

Jesus was a good guy but he got distracted with the resurrection cult that was popular during his time. The cult had been established in Egypt many centuries earlier and Jesus became indoctrinated when he travelled there. He never died on the cross as some books would have you believe. There was a poor fellow named Barabbas that took his place. When the switch was made, the body of

Barabbas was whisked away and buried in an unmarked grave and then Jesus stepped in to make it appear he had risen from the dead. The apostles were aware of the ruse and played along since the theme was important to the cause as was the symbolism. The resurrection was nicely played.

Jesus had an important message and he delivered effectively but because of the whole "son of god" thing that was written in centuries later, the point was lost and the message became distorted.

Frankly, what Jesus was trying to say could have been much better portrayed had his words been preserved properly. He was certainly an advanced mind/body/spirit complex and chose to come back to this plane of existence to help out. It was many hundreds of years later after Jesus and his wife had passed that his words were distorted and meaning changed in order to make him the so-called son of the Jewish god Yahweh."

"Wait a minute," I said. "Did you just say that Jesus was married?"

"Of course. I thought that it was pretty clear even in the distorted text that you call the bible. Jesus and Mary were husband and wife, how else could they have travelled together? The records even talk about their wedding in Cana.

You can imagine how Enlil and I had a good chuckle when we found out that Jesus was portrayed as the son of god and the god that had been picked was Yahweh. We thought that everyone on earth would see that as a pretty good joke. Imagine our surprise when we discovered everyone believed it.

People have to understand that the Old Testament was copied from previously written works. The exploits of the early Sumerian civilization as captured on the clay tablets found in Iraq at the turn of the last century is a more accurate reflection of the history of gods and man.

How do I know this? I pretty much directed the writing of the clay cylinders and tablets. So I know the Sumerian texts were written first and what you call the Old Testament in your bible came later and drew heavily from the Sumerian texts.

The so called gospels of the New Testament were written 30 – 70 years after Jesus died and Paul's letters were written earlier. But the entire text was manipulated and rewritten many times to foster the growth of a powerful organization.

Jesus was not in any way related to Jehovah or connected to the Sumerian civilization for that matter. He was an advanced mind/body/soul with a specific task to enlighten mankind. He utilized the power that is within everyone to heal plus he taught and performed many amazing feats. Some were real and some were made up.

Jesus' message was simple. We are all gods, we are all one and we have all come from the same source: The One Infinite Creator. We are in The Creator and The Creator is in us so that we can experience all things possible and that includes the power of love. That's it, a message that should have grown and captivated humans, but instead it became the basis for war and barbarism.

He even talked about a wide road to destruction and a narrow road to heaven. Does this not sound like maybe he was talking about positively polarized path versus the negative one?

Look at what Jesus was trying to say in today's terms. Think of what he said 2000 years ago in a completely different cultural setting only filter it through the eyes of modern man. Read between the lines knowing that the supposed words in your modern text come from later edits added long after he was dead."

"You seem to know a lot about Jesus," I suggested.

"That is correct, but let's not dwell on what Jesus tried to tell you. I will tell you more about how I know him, later. Instead let's talk about where you humans are now.

You think that you are highly evolved beings in an advanced world with the technology to communicate, calculate and entertain. You think that technology has made your life easier because you can put your clothes in a machine and press a button and put dishes in another machine with another button. Buying stuff from a computer and having it delivered to your home without leaving your couch seems like the pinnacle has been reached.

I am here to say that you are not highly evolved at all. Your choice in an evolutionary path has taken you to various crossroads. Each and every time you have chosen the hardest path, the one that takes you further and further away from advancing to 4th density.

You must work mundane and boring jobs in order to heat your houses to keep from freezing to death in the winter. The plains Indians sitting around a warm fire in their tepees' 200 years ago were more spiritually advanced than you are today.

Each day you trudge off to the factory to work in conditions far worse than we ever exposed you to in the mines. Don't forget, I fashioned Homo-sapien to dig gold in the mines of Africa and I can tell you most assuredly that you were treated better 5000 years ago than you are today in your steel factories, pulp mills and cement plants.

You can create new circumstances and exciting situations in your lives but instead you would rather watch those things happen to actors on TV or in the movies.

You can directly communicate with each other but you would rather pay a telecommunication company fees so that you can hold one of their clever devices to your head with the same function that was your gift from the beginning. Do you not think that you have the ability to communicate with whoever you choose whenever you want?

If you want to go somewhere, you must crawl into a tube with wings, accompanied by many others, while consuming hundreds of tonnes of fuel. Can you imagine how inefficient this is when quite frankly, like in your dreams, you could have chosen to fly on your own?

The human race has always chosen the difficult path and it has led you to a world of concrete, steel, silicon and oil. You are not the advanced civilization that you think. This is a backwards world in the backwoods of the galaxy. You are the hillbillies, as they say, of the Milky Way and yet you have deluded yourselves into thinking that you are advanced. It will be another thousand years before you are ready to set out and start to explore the galaxy, Star Trek style.

I can tell you that there are advanced civilizations in 3rd, 4th, and 5th density that have explored all corners of the universe on a light beam. They can think anything they desire into existence and know exactly who they are and where they have come from and where they are going.

Others travel by thought and to think you too had the choice for this kind of development.

Unfortunately, most humans can't get past first base and don't know who they are to begin with. You might say this is because of the veil but let me offer you this one observation. As long as you have religion as the basis for belief, you will continue to flounder and be the so-called backwater of the galaxy. Is that a correct term, backwater?"

"Um, well, maybe, I guess." I weakly replied.

"Good, then you will stagnate for thousands of years as you continually reincarnate and miss the point.

That was what Jesus was trying to tell you silly people. He had to speak in so-called parables in order to adhere to the first directive of non-interference but the message, we thought, was loud and clear.

If you realize that you are infinite beings and that you are on a journey of self-discovery then you will continue to evolve and understand your value. If you acknowledge that you are all in it together and come from the same source, then you can start to make decisions en masse that will move your evolution along exponentially.

I have said that the veil sped up your evolution but your ignorance has slowed it down.

So we come back to the choice and I suppose everyone can look around and see that there are people who do good and people who do bad. But most folks don't realize that the choice to do good or evil comes down to whether you choose to serve self or serve others. Everything else comes from that choice. Then the harvest occurs and those marked for 4th density positive all go one way and those qualifying for negative work go the other."

"This is getting a little more interesting now," I said. "So tell me what 4th density positive looks like."

"Fourth density positive is where the concept of love is explored. In 3rd density the idea of love is misconstrued, distorted or plain misunderstood. Yes, love is the feeling that a man may have for a woman and vice versa but it is much more than that. Love for oneself, love for mankind and unconditional love are all 3rd density concepts that only scratch the surface. To give you an idea of the depth of the concept of love, it typically takes a mind/body/spirit complex about 2 million revolutions of your earth around the sun to accomplish all the tasks and learning of the 4th density love field."

"Did you say 2 million years?"

"Yes 2 million years is about what it takes to learn the concepts.

So, let's talk about what 4th density looks like. First, it is this earth that will become home to 4th density positively polarized entities because the earth herself is transitioning to 4th density.

Everyone from 3rd density will die as you do now but only those reincarnating in 4th density positive will come back here, to the earth plane. Those repeating 3rd density, will reincarnate elsewhere and those going on to 4th density negative will also go elsewhere, a planet that is specific for negative work.

So you must realize by now that the 3rd density earth plane with its primary purpose being one of choice allows for negative and positive people to co-mingle thereby giving each the opportunity to explore the opposing paths.

With this information you should no longer ponder the senselessness of war or suffering or anything else that happens on earth. It should be clear that it is no more than an illusion or what you might call a virtual reality training program for infinite beings. It allows infinite beings to express how they choose to return to the Creator. Those who are in the process of choosing the positive path will be the servers while those on the negative track will be the controllers. It's really quite simple when you boil it down.

Therefore, the earth will become a 4th density planet for 4th density beings to do 4th density positive work. Children that are being born now to 3rd density parents and are ready for 4th density work are special hybrids. They are the ones that already qualify for 4th density work and want to be here during the transition. They have dual chemical complexes that are ready for activation to 4th density ensuring them a spot in the new world. I call it dual citizenship.

They are born with 3rd and 4th density bodies with 3rd density sitting in the forefront and 4th density waiting in behind. They will be the first beings to populate the planet when the earth transitions. This is quite important because right now some are able to move back and forth between 3rd and 4th density bodies. The unique part about assuming your 4th density body while still in a 3rd density environment is that one is invisible to the other. A 3rd density being cannot see a 4th density being."

"Why is that Enki," I asked.

"It is because 4th density beings have chosen for it to be this way," he replied.

Entities born before your timekeeping date of 1986 will die and then reincarnate to 4th density bodies providing that they qualify on the positive side. It's because they were born with 3rd density bodies like everyone else for the past 10,000 years. If however you were born after the reckoning date of 1986 and were qualified for 4th density positive work then you may have been born with the dual chemical complex body and will easily transcend the shift during the earth changes. These entities will still experience a typical 3rd density death but now the transition to 4th density will be much easier.

If you were born after 1986 and were qualified for 4th density negative work, then you probably would have been born with a normal chemical complex body and the transitional reincarnation would take place elsewhere on a 4th density negative planet. Same for those who have not made the choice yet and are inbetween negative and positive polarities such that they too will reincarnate on another 3rd density planet elsewhere.

So you see that earth has been set aside for 4th density positive work which is the labour of love, sort of speak. You probably also realize that the changes are slow and you are in the midst of them now. The Mayan Calendar fooled everyone into thinking that the earth's changes were going to happen quickly, one day perhaps, but no, that is not the case. These changes are happening ever so slowly but rest assured they are happening."

"Well yes, it would certainly seem so based on what you have said so far." I replied, hoping not to sound too negatively inclined. "But, you could be feeding me a cock and bull story about the meaning of life and there is nothing really to substantiate anything you have said in any way, shape or form.

I find myself at a crossroad as to whether to believe that you are an authentic god, Sumerian or otherwise or a raving lunatic. I mean that in the nicest possible way and quite respectfully. But since there are people in the world that would beguile and confuse as willingly as educate and illuminate, it seems there is no way of knowing one from the other. So how do you tell? That was rhetorical by the way.

I am left with that crazy old concept that I read all the time from both those who feel they are sharing genuine information and the crackpots who want a bit of attention. You must let your heart determine the sense of truthfulness. Does it ring true deep inside and resonate with your being?

What a crock of shit, I say. Show me proof. Now you did take me on a little journey and showed me energy forms of solid matter but that only confirms what Einstein already knew, matter and energy are interchangeable. Our scientists have learned a great deal about quantum physics and understand the interaction between particles and energy and that it appears as if they are one and the same.

How you were able to show me these things, I am at a loss.

You have told me that you were here at the beginning of our earth history as a visitor from another planet and have given me descriptions of what that looked like some 10,000 years ago. Maybe it was, maybe it wasn't.

But without a doubt, you have given me a tremendous amount of information, the kind that I would have difficulty sharing with friends and family, that is, if I want them to continue to think of me as a sane person. You see, there appears to be a fine line between nut-bar and god. So, bottom line, what do you want from me?"

"Nothing," Enki replied. "But you may want something from me. You are at a crossroad of your evolution and advancement to 4th density hangs in the balance since you have been in 3rd density for many incarnations. You are close to graduating but not quite there yet.

It is time for you to move on to the next density and someone needs to give you a nudge. If I give you information that helps you understand who you are, then use it or throw it out. In general, if I can teach one person that they are more than they could ever imagine and that they are here to make a choice and advance, then I will have succeeded.

Sometimes it only takes one to make a difference. But here is my bottom line. There is a harvest coming and I have information regarding that event. I am telling you and others that are ready for advancement that existence in this world is about making a choice and if you reincarnate 10,000 times it is for only one reason. It is to choose your path back to the One Infinite Creator.

You have also been granted free will in this system and to make free will worthwhile you need to forget everything about who you really are and where you come from in order to quicken your evolution. You must experience each successive lifetime to progressively awaken under the forgetting condition until the great cycle comes to an end. Hopefully you will have woken up enough to smell the roses.

Then those who are ready to move on will move and those who are not will continue with 3rd density learning. Same goes for 2nd density beings. They too must progress so they can become ready for 3rd density work when harvest time comes around."

"Wow, hang on a sec. You've only mentioned 2nd density beings once before so let's talk about that for a moment. Who or what are 2nd density beings again and what determines their degree of evolution?"

"I thought I might get your attention with that one. Perhaps the best example of a 2nd density being that is ready to graduate to 3rd density is the family pet. A domestic dog that is gentle and kind around the kids and greets everyone enthusiastically with its tail wagging and is quite happy to be around people.

Another example of 2nd density beings ready to enter 3rd density are trees. They are kind gentle giants who have waited patiently for thousands of years to transition. Their great strength is their patience. They do not war, nor do they judge. They happily provide a service to humans by making themselves available for construction purposes and other such uses. These entities are highly polarized towards service to others and at the end of the cycle will move up to 3rd density and in this special case they will be the only 3rd density entities allowed to remain on earth once the great mother makes her transition. Other 2nd density beings that do not transition with the harvest will stay here as well.

Do not miss-judge the beings you call trees as they are very powerful 2nd density beings and have great abilities. They choose to stand stoic and majestic and have no spiteful or negative intentions which you can be thankful for. They will retain their same basic form in 4th density.

I have seen other worlds where these beings have not been so pleasant. They had literally mowed down and eliminated 3rd density life. Had these kind trees come to populate this planet, I can assure you, they would have killed every last one of you efficiently and effectively. Quite ornery indeed, and of course, negatively polarised.

Now let me remind you again that the One Infinite Creator created the Logos, one of which is the Central Galactic Sun of the so-called "Milky Way". The Logos created the sub-Logos, one of which the Sun in this solar system is a part. The Sun of this solar system created sub-sub-Logos of which you are a part. Each successive part has been endowed with the ability to create, so do you see, it all makes sense, the One Infinite Creator is you, and you are him.

He seeks to experience all of his creation through what he has created and then gives his creation the same ability so you become co-creators in all that is. But I say again, you are not meant to know every detail at this point since you might already begin to ponder whether a worm creates the dirt that it lives in.

You are here to maximize your experiences and to make the choice. The choice defines your path back to the One Infinite Creator and gives you your marching orders for the next 10 billion years. Now do you see how important this concept is?"

"Surely I do my friend." I replied. "The concept of polarity boils down to the simple idea of service to self as being negative and service to others as positive. Everything else falls inside of those two concepts such as good and evil, angel and devil, hot and cold, black and white and Vladimir Putin and Barak Obama.

The world is a funny place Enki, and as much as I want to believe you, it is hard, but the concepts are clear. The New Testament says believe in Jesus, the son of god and you shall have everlasting life. If you choose not to believe then you shall find eternal damnation in hell.

Now you come along and say choose the negative path or choose the positive path in order to move on with your evolution. If you get wishy-washy about the whole thing you get regurgitated a couple of million times until you get it. The catch is that most don't even know there is a decision to be made. How do I know this is the ticket?"

"You don't," replied Enki. "But if you look at all the ancient literature, esoteric and occult writings and even some modern history you will find a common thread throughout. Surely you noticed that the Sun (Son) was important because the ancient Egyptians worshipped it.

The Babylonians also worshipped the Sun as did the Aztecs and Incas. The sun is the son of the One Infinite Creator.

Christians worship the Son and it was the Son that said "I am in the father and the father is in me". Now just interject the One Infinite Creator in place of the father and apply it to all living beings and you have the greatest truth mankind could ever know and this is what Jesus was trying to say before it got distorted. The Sun is the Son.

The Buddha saw clearly the reincarnated aspect of this illusion and taught it to his pupils. Thoth uttered some of the most profound saying for mankind to unravel and his best was "As above so below, as below so above." This means that all microcosms are part of a macrocosm and all macrocosms are part of a microcosm.

You might ask yourself why an atom with its electrons in orbit around the nucleus resembles the Sun with its planets orbiting in a likewise fashion?

Thoth, who was called Ningishzidda in Sumeria, was my son and is with me here on Earth today to help carry out this work. Ningishzidda actually came up with the key ingredient in our genetic splicing experiments which was the break-through in the creation of modern Homo-sapien. So you see, he too has a special interest in seeing you silly fellows on to the next step."

"Well, you certainly are not short on surprises," I replied. "Although I believe you did mention earlier that Thoth was your son, I didn't know he was kicking about here on earth doing god stuff. Maybe we can go for a beer someday, the three of us and can you imagine what my friends would say? You had a beer with Enki aka the lord god Jehovah and Ningishzidda aka Thoth, totally crazy man?

It does make sense what you have said about Buddha and Jesus, I am just not sure what I am supposed to do.

Should I start writing science fiction books and then start a religion that has famous movie stars as members to help attract attention.

Maybe I should look at golden plates through crystal rocks in a paper bag and write a book.

Maybe I can base a new religion on some guy that lived a long time ago where there were rumours that his mom was a virgin and his dad was a god. His name was Achilles if you recall.

However, I am now seeing your point. I could go out and actually attract a following since there are enough people around ready to buy into almost anything. We live in a crazy time I must say. "

"OK, I will leave you with these ideas to digest for a little while and then later I suggest we visit a 4th density planet so that you get the idea of what I am talking about."

"Huh, what?" I stammered. "Visit a 4th density planet?? How are we supposed to do that? Are you going to pick me up on a space ship? Can I have a window seat?"

"Funny you should say that," replied Enki. "We did that, about 5000 years ago when we first came to earth, established our colony and successfully created the human species.

There was one particular chap whom I named Adapa. He was actually the Adam that was referred to in the bible but he was the product of the union of myself and an existing earth woman, which I told you about earlier.

Adapa was so gifted and intelligent that my brother Enlil and I both agreed (one of the few times) that he should come back to Nibiru and meet our father Anu. It was a disaster but that's another story.

So, we will go to a 4th density planet but before we do I want to impress upon you that there are many ways to travel and many ways to explore worlds so I will show you a different method than perhaps you are used to.

 I will meet you one night in your dreams and I will implore you to follow me on the journey that will take us to the other worlds. But I need you to leave yourself with suggestions every night before going to sleep. This is almost the same as a hypnotic suggestion but you are asking your inner self to help achieve the goal of intergalactic travel. Dreams are extremely difficult to manipulate for an outsider such as me and I will definitely need help from your inner self."

"OK, you've successfully confused me again," I replied. "You need help from my inner self, a part of me that until a couple of weeks ago, I didn't know existed. What do you want me to do or say? Not another one of those rhymes I hope."

"All you need to say is that I give permission to travel with the entity known as Enki. If he is an imposter or if he does not have my best interests in mind, then no deal. That's it, as your inner self will know my true intents. If you are OK with that, then let's begin tonight as it will take time for the energies to align."

"OK, I'll do it," I said. "Only because of our previous experience with the energy stuff and quite frankly, I am actually starting to like this strange shit and believe it or not, I am starting to like you too. But how is it again that we will travel?"

"We will travel with our dreaming bodies."

CHAPTER 7: THE DREAMING BODY AND LIFE AS A MOVIE

The little exercise Enki had given me to help travel in my dreaming body, was taken quite seriously. After all, who wouldn't want to get a real cool trip to another planet?

Then one day, I actually said this out loud and it sounded like I was in need of help, serious mental help. It took virtually no effort however to say a couple of silly things to myself before going to bed at night. I just didn't want to mumble them out loud and have my wife institutionalize me.

I had not seen Enki either at the coffee shop or in my dreams for several weeks and wondered if he was off trying to make someone else crazy. Then as fate would have it or as I fearfully suspected, Enki was waiting for the right time and place to reappear in my life to turn it upside down again.

I was in a sports store checking out the new line of golf clubs when from behind I heard that familiar accented voice say....

"Hello there."

I turned around and said, "Hey Enki, how ya dooin?"

"Good thanks," he replied. "I have been working with your inner self at a deeper level to set up our trip but it has occurred to me that there is some more information that I need to give you in order for the energies to align."

"Wonderful," I replied. "I haven't been blasted off my feet for at least a couple of weeks now with crazy wild-ass ideas, nor have I been in the presence of a god for a while either."

"Consider yourself lucky then," Enki replied. "Because if it had been my brother Enlil that had got the job of informing mankind of imminent changes, he would have already jammed a lightning bolt up your ass for being insolent. He took that god stuff seriously you know."

"Riiiiiight," I said.

"OK, so there is some missing information in your little pea brain that needs to be incorporated in order for our work to continue. I realized after having a conversation with your inner self that you do not have a complete understanding of the whole self. You do not yet have the ability to imagine yourself in a different place at a different time.

It's the imagination that fuels the ability to travel the way I would like us to travel and yours is not developed enough to accomplish this. I might liken your imagination to that of a gnat so I need to tell you a bit more about yourself."

"Thanks for the vote of confidence by the way."

"No problem. To do this, I have scanned some recent memories of dreams you have had to develop the tools for us to complete the journey.

So to start I need you to understand that you are a multi-dimensional being. One who exists in several worlds at the same time. Your inner self is an oversoul as they say and although you and your inner self are one and the same, the other selves or other portions of yourself are also one and the same. You exist right now in three different worlds as seven different people but you are all one entity, if that makes sense.”

“Oh yeah, that makes perfect sense,” I replied as I rolled my eyes.

“Good, then I will relay to you a dream you had recently that you should remember, which will verify to you that I have been in contact with your inner self who is the maker of dreams.

You had a dream where you were in a plot to kill several people and then escape with a certain sum of money. You were plotting with a number of other people and there was a master plan that was in process. The only problem was that you had forgotten what the plan was and you were a little confused when you arrived at the site where the murder/robbery was to take place.

Instead of remembering the official plan, you ad-libbed by killing the culprit and absconded with the money, not exactly according to plan, but good enough for an impromptu alternative. You then realized that the dead body was in need of being discarded and you needed to exit the country pronto. So you buried the body and took the cash and set out to find a way to Mexico. Sound familiar?”

Quite incredulously and with a stupid open-mouth look of amazement I said, “Yeah. It was a dream I had had a few nights ago.”

“Well then,” Enki went on. “You should also be familiar with a dream about a month earlier in which you were running from the police and found yourself in an old farmyard. Although this dream happened in a time prior to the one I just described, the sequence in which it happened was just the opposite.

So you are running from the law and they have you trapped in a farm yard. You run in front of an old barn and the bullets are hitting the barn all around as you run. You then get inside the barn and work your way up to a ledge on the outside of the barn only to find that a detective has followed you up to the very edge on which you stand.

There is nowhere else to run and you are out of bullets so the agent points his gun at you and tells you that it is finished. You look at him and tell him that it is not finished until it is finished and open your coat.

Inside you are carrying a bomb strapped to your body and the detonator is in your hand. You look at the policeman as his eyes go wide and you think to yourself, I wonder what this is going to feel like" then you press the button. Remember this one?"

I was flabbergasted as not only did I remember both dreams but I had written them down in my journal. Enki had described the dreams almost word for word.

"How did you know that?" I asked incredulously.

"I scanned your dream memory with permission from your inner self which of course is you, in order to garner this information. More importantly however, the dream is about another part of you which is living another life at another time. But since time outside of this construct does not exist as you know it, you and your other selves are living simultaneous lives. His name is Phil and he is working on a particular set of life objectives, as are you."

"Yeah but what kind of person is this Phil?" I said rather obnoxiously. "I don't go around killing other people so how do you expect me to believe I am that same person?"

"Well, you hunt don't you? You kill animals, right? What makes you think animals are any less important than humans? All living things are sacred and immortal which is, in one form or another, the Creator experiencing himself. So you kill another human or you kill a deer, it is all the same and is equivalent to killing yourself.

Very simply, that is what we call it the law of one which states that we are all the same in the One Infinite Creator. So when you kill another living thing you kill a portion of the creator which is a portion of yourself.

It is the concept you must understand not the act since a deer will become a deer again, if it chooses and a human will become a human again if he or she chooses. There are lessons to be learned, experiences to be experienced along with growth and advancement.

Take for example the person that was killed by Phil in order to gain the sum of money that was in the suitcase. Phil was enacting the plan before he and his victim came into the construct. It was done this way for a multitude of reasons and was acted perfectly according to plan. At any point either Phil or the other fellow could have made free will decisions to avoid the occurrence but they marched on to the tune of what was pre-arranged and was of benefit to both.

Don't forget, neither you nor anyone else in the universe can destroy an entity that is part of the Creator. You will always exist.

The deer that you killed last fall was in no way less important than the person Phil killed. A deer is the One Infinite Creator and the Creator was experiencing himself as a deer. The deer may have starved to death that winter, may have been eaten alive by wolves or may have gone on to live many more cycles. The deer was not destroyed but will continue to reincarnate as a deer until it is ready to graduate to 3rd density.

The point of this exercise is to show you that you are a multi-dimensional being and you dance with all life forms whether you are here or a 100 billion light years from here. Situations that help with your growth experience are put together and agreed upon by all those involved.

You help others and in return receive help. Only those on the negative path find it sometimes lonely as service to self often only requires the services of the self. Other negative entities seek to dominate and control when it comes to interacting with others. But don't feel sorry for these types as it is a path freely chosen and it is the only other legitimate way to experience life on the journey back to the Creator.

Think of life as a movie in which you are the producer, director and lead actor. You have invited several close associates to take part as supporting actors and actresses to help with the production.

The movie is then written, acted and filmed according to the script that you wrote. With all your close friends ready, willing and able to play the parts they have been asked to play everyone immerses themselves into their roles.

Some actors in Hollywood get so involved in their character that lines blur between who they are and who the character is that they are playing. And so do you, mostly because you are supposed to forget who you are.

On top of that, you have agreed to play support roles for others in their own movies and whether it be a cameo appearance or a support role, your part is important to the entity that you support. That support role that you play may take place on this planet or another; it may take place in a different area of your present world or at a completely different period of time.

Anything is possible as you may lead several lives during different time periods or several lives all at the same time but in different places, like you and Phil for example. That's what I mean when I say you are multi-dimensional.

In your dream as Phil, you are playing a support role for a very close friend that has been with you for thousands of years. You have supported each other in almost of all your important lives. When you dream of yourself as Phil this is a bleed-through from that life and it shouldn't surprise you that sometimes Phil dreams of you in this life."

"Who is this person that Phil is working with? Do I know him/her in my present life here and now?" I asked in a moment of genuine intrigue.

"Unfortunately I can't share that information with you as it would obstruct the law of free will," Enki replied. "In other words it may affect decisions you make towards this person in this life which you may otherwise not have made.

So, you are the main character in this present life and you have invited many to support your cause. You have come here to learn a very important part of who you are and to use that as a catapult into 4th density.

This life that you lead today is the most important of all the hundreds of lives you have had on earth previously and it is positioning you for fourth density work. You have asked many entities to support you in this cause and each has been instrumental in your success. You are just about there.

Your wife has had the most important role as she has shown you the right-hand path. Even though she has been with you from the beginning, you were dense and not able to see the value in what she was teaching you. You had to explore the left-hand path and see for yourself what that looked like. Yes, it was exotic and exciting but it was not the path you had chosen for yourself to return to the One Infinite Creator.

It was the right-hand path that is yours to follow, the one that your wife was so entrenched in and you only needed to 'see' her to see the path. So now that you have seen both paths, it is time for you to decide and that is why I am talking to you. It is the reason I am here, to help those that are close to finishing 3rd density. You need to decide your path and then take the definitive steps to establish the course. Once done, you will be free to graduate."

"Well, that was a bit intense," I replied. "But it is a little strange to me that if I am so close to harvest, as you say, why is it so difficult to understand the whole game. Especially when we forget who we are and what we are doing here."

"I've told you this before," Enki went on. "This density is not one for the accumulation of knowledge, which is why the forgetting is so effective. You are not supposed to know everything. You are supposed to feel and experience things. Some will never know nor understand what I have told you but they will still graduate to fourth density because they are in service to others instinctively and wholeheartedly. They grasp the idea without knowing the concept, they feel, they live, they experience and most importantly they love.

Others just exist and go on with the drudgery of life, never revelling in a sunset, never smelling a flower or pondering the greatness of the universe. In other words they cannot feel or experience the deepness and richness of life. They are just barely alive and go about their daily business in a vacuous trance of unknowing, perpetuating a meaningless cycle of reincarnation. All are on a journey but it takes some longer than others."

That night and for many nights thereafter, I religiously cited my incantation on my dream-body to push for the acceptance to travel to another world with Enki. I continually asked my inner self to give me guidance and to allow Enki to take me on a journey.

I was a bit of a risk taker anyways so it was not so much of a stretch for me to dream my ass to another sector of the galaxy. Then one night I fell asleep with the usual thoughts running through my thick skull when someone in a hazy fog with a familiar voice said....

"Hi Jim, do you know who I am? Do you recognize me?"

Chapter 8: Other Worlds.

There were two realizations that had come upon me simultaneously. The first was that I had fallen asleep and was dreaming while the second was that I appeared to be awake in my dream.

 I seemed to know I was dreaming and I had brought along my waking consciousness with me into the dream. Normal dreaming for me had always been a hazy, fuzzy world in which strange things happened and I was sometimes a participant and sometimes an observer but there was always a sense that it was unreal. It's like when you recognize someone but they are unfamiliar at the same time.

Despite the sense of fantasy, it never occurred to me in my dreams that I was dreaming. Now however it was as real as if Enki was standing beside me.

"Yes," I replied. "You are my friend Enki, the guy who thinks he is Yahweh."

"Well done," he said. "Let's do a small exercise to see if you are ready. I am going to float up above the buildings so why don't you follow me."

As he said the words, I could see Enki slowly lifting off the ground and float upwards towards the top of the buildings just as he described. I closed my eyes for a moment and imagined the same happening to me and then I became light-headed.

I opened my eyes and sure enough I had achieved lift-off and I was floating from street level, upwards past the +15 connectors that linked building to building. I floated past the lower apartments until finally I had cleared the tallest office building.

I wasn't freaked out at all since I knew this was a dream and nothing permanently bad can happen in a dream. Besides, it was my will that was causing me to rise up and explore the heights so I would have to be an idiot to reverse that and plummet back down to earth.

"So here we are about to have another conversation," I said. "Only difference is that we are 600m above the street and looking down at the tops of the buildings. Does that not seem odd to you?"

"Not at all," Enki replied. "I have conversations up here all the time. It is important to realize however that you are up here in your other body, your dream body. Rest assured, this body is every bit as real as the one lying in bed right now plus you have gained new appreciation for it and other aspects of yourself in one bold move.

You are up here of your own free will and have now learned to power your dream body using your will or that part of you that exists as consciousness. You have merely transferred it from one body to another. Do you understand what I am saying?"

"I think so," I replied. "I have transferred my consciousness into this other body that is light and capable of ...... well let's see."

As I said those words I began to think of fast movement through the air. I positioned my body in a traditional superman pose, then, just like that I shot off into the night. If I twisted my body to the right, I went right. If I wanted to go up or down it didn't matter, whatever I thought of doing, or however fast I thought of going was immediately implemented. It was like Cpt. Jean-Luc Picard saying 'make it so'."

Enki was right beside me the whole way, laughing and cracking jokes at how poorly I was flying. Meanwhile we were dodging in-between buildings, going straight up the face of one and down another at what seemed like excessive speeds. I wondered if there were dream cops up here with radar guns.

"Now it would seem that you are ready to take a journey of great magnitude," Enki said. "But before we do that, let's see how well you adjust to travel by thought. We are going to take a small trip to the planet that you call Mars as I want to show you something very interesting.

Mars has a history that you may not know as it was once an outpost of ours which we used as a way station for the transportation of gold back to Nibiru. It was manned by fellow Annunaki during a time when Mars had an atmosphere and a normal but slightly harsh climate. Are you ready to go?"

"Sure," I replied in a faraway voice. "Why not Mars."

"OK then, I want you to hold on to my hand and when you feel a slight jolt like an electric shock you will seem a little bewildered followed by something like being drawn into a vacuum. Again, this is normal and I am explaining it to you now so you will not be surprised or freak out. This is how we travel very long distances in short order. OK?"

"Got it," I replied. "After all I have been through with you so far, why should I freak out."

Enki then reached out and grabbed my hand and true to form, I was jolted by what seemed like a shock and then I was sucked into a vortex of swirling turbulence and harsh vibration.

I opened my eyes after a split second and found myself leaving the atmosphere of earth at an excessive speed straight out into space. The feeling was somewhat strange to be sure but I did not feel like I needed to panic. Enki still had my hand and for some reason this seemed to be OK and I felt safe. Within a blink, we were on solid ground, standing and looking out over a very bleak and unassuming landscape.

"I take it this is Mars," I said rather obliquely.

"Right you are," Enki replied. "This was my home for about a year of your earth time, long long ago but as you can see, it has become very inhospitable over time. There used to be an atmosphere on Mars but now it is barren and void of any life as you can see. What do you think?"

"Well," I stammered. "Bleak is an understatement but how is it that we can stand here without the need for protection from the cold and solar radiation? I'm sure there is some hefty solar radiation going on. What is protecting us?"

"Your question comes from a place of misunderstanding," Enki replied. "What you fail to understand is that your dream body differs vastly from your chemical body back on earth. You do not need protection, or air, or sustenance. The dream body is not built like that. It is fuelled by the all-encompassing universal energy that emanates from the central galactic sun which draws its source from the One Infinite Creator."

Enki was right. Not only did my body feel light and energetic but my mind was fully alert and conscious of everything around me so it seemed like the right time to ask a question that had been bothering me for some time.

"Enki," I started. "I'd like to ask a question that has been on my mind for some time. There just does not seem to be an answer and while we were sitting here on the planet Mars, I thought we might have a chat."

"Sure Jim, shoot." Replied Enki, confident that he had all the answers.

"OK. I have a friend who went through a really devastating situation where he lost his son. My friend never really recovered from the trauma and it destroyed the family. The boy who was killed never had a chance to grow and experience life as it was cut short at the age of 3. Why do things like this happen? What possible good could come from something like this?"

"First of all, you have to realize that the focus is wrong. The boy is fine and already back in the world in another body and another life."

Enki seemed to know the situation I was talking about.

"The correct way to look at this situation is how the event affected your friend. It devastated him as you stated. But there is more.

The child dies but in reality you may look at this as a spirit entity fulfilling its purpose and commitment to another spirit entity in providing catalyst for learning and growth."

"What kind of learning could a situation like this possibly provide, Enki?"

"It is twofold my friend. First, it is an awakening. Second it provides balance.

Traumatic situations like this cause an individual to question everything about life. It overwhelms one to the point of obsessively seeking answers to questions that are impossible to answer. This seeking often leads to many realizations which always cause deep contemplation. It is then that the exploration of self begins.

Balancing however deals with energies on the karmic level and usually extend over many lives and incarnations. An entity may have become unbalanced through a series of tragic events over several lifetimes. The current tragedy allows the entity to balance out the emotions, energies and feeling brought forward from past events.

When an entity has had many lives of misdirection, this can lead to a fulcrum that is off centre or an unbalanced beam where the fulcrum is right but the weight on either end differs. Just like a teeter totter with a fat kid on one end and a skinny kid on the other. The fat kid is symbolic of guilt, say, while the skinny kid represents inadequacy. In terms of emotions, these could be left over from previous lives which have never been dealt with.

The entity in question then plans out an especially difficult life in which he/she intends to deal with, and balance out the emotions. If forgiveness is involved, it quite often gets misconstrued as the need to forgive others when in fact it is forgiveness of self that is required.

This sets up the drama for a traumatic event such as your friend's death experience of his son. The catalyst for self-forgiveness is then set in motion. Usually, the untimely death of a son or daughter has to do with self-forgiveness."

"OK, Enki, maybe I buy that line of reasoning, but what if the person does not see the meaning or grasp the implications of the event as you have explained. They haven't awakened nor understood the learning intended. What happens then?"

"Usually the entity sets up these situations inbetween incarnations. He/she enlists friends and family to help and it is this help that is critical to the success of the situation. It may take many years and different events unfolding to help the individual deal with the resolution of the karmic energies.

The thickness of skin as you say, may sometimes cause the individual to not see the learning at all. Over time, unfortunately, the effect of catalyst dulls and is eventually forgotten."

"What happens then, Enki?"

"The entity is into a do-over."

"What does that mean?"

"It means that the importance of resolving the karmic imbalance does not go away when the entity dies.

The entity is still faced with the problem in the spirit state and will seek to resolve it in a similar fashion in a new life. He will go through the same difficult situation in his next life and encounter the same feelings all over again.

This time however, the entity will enlist even more help to ensure he gets it right. The death of a son or daughter will be acted out again and the experience will be repeated. The entity will be more careful in planning to ensure success the next time.

These lives are difficult and not many entities want to repeat these kinds of events."

"But Enki, do we not have another catch 22? The veil is supposed to prevent us from knowing our true selves but you are saying we have to pierce the veil in order to understand and resolve these situations."

"Yes, but don't forget, you have had the benefit of thousands of years of teaching from such enlightened entities as Buddha and Jesus. Even of late, your teachings of the past 4 decades have increased your knowledge tremendously.

There was Seth and Juan Matus in the '70's, Ra in the 80's and now you have me. There can be no excuses anymore.

The veil is slowly being lifted for those who care to notice since the harvest is beckoning."

"OK, I get it, but let's get back to the original problem. Is it better to realize the meaning of a traumatic event early after the event has happened or later after much thought and the raw edge has worn off?"

"It is always better to deal with it as early as possible. The dreams that come after such an event always prompt one to start almost at once. Dreams or perhaps a better term is nightmares, remind the entity of the event and the immediate need to deal with it. The circumstances of the trauma are replayed in many different symbolic forms designed specifically to give clues as to the nature of the event and the healing that is required.

For instance, in your friend's case, the issue is self-forgiveness. Dreams could contain such religious symbols as the Christ figure bleeding on the cross or a blood soaked lamb all pointing towards forgiveness if in fact the entity was religiously orientated.

 If not, non-religious symbols would be used such as murderers confronting the parents of the deceased or olive branches being offered to those that have been wronged. Another symbol often used is the dove. All of these are then mixed with blood, death and horror to impress upon the dreamer the importance of dealing with the situation.

Nightmares can go on like this for years, continually causing stress during the waking hours and even terror at the thought of going to sleep at night. By design, the nightmares prompt and force the entity to find a solution.

But after a long time, the dreams do fade and the opportunity for learning and enlightenment fade along with them.

Sometimes a second tragic event is needed later in life so that the new tragedy becomes linked to the old. The dreams start over and the entity is forced to relive the old while dealing with the new. Catalyst becomes unbearable until healing is sought and brought about.

This is a hard lesson and the crucible in which it is learned is searing hot. Not many want to incur this more than in one life.

The veil is slowly lifted for those who are ready to see. And for those who do not, well, there is another 75,000 year cycle ready to go.

You might think of it as going to college. If you flunk out in your first year because you drank too much beer and skipped too many classes then there is always next year where you can repeat and hopefully not screw up. You see, life is full of symbols."

As we sat there and talked, the irony of our situation had not been lost on me. Here we were sitting on the planet Mars, me and a supposed Sumerian god, talking about the things that affect life on Earth and the people who live there. We weren't even in our regular bodies and talking about how painful it can be with what we experience as humans.

We sat in silence for a few minutes and while I was contemplating the reasonableness of what Enki had just said, I was sure he was contemplating his next move.

Then after what seemed like a lifetime, we set off on a sightseeing tour around Mars looking at all the odd sights while Enki explained how the planet had been used by the Annunaki during the early days as a wayward station to transfer gold back to the home planet. It was all very fascinating and hard to imagine that anything was real anymore.

Then with a jolt we were off again at breakneck speed to another world that Enki promised I would love. He called it an early 3rd density world and explained to me how my world might have developed along these lines had the Annunaki not interfered with our evolution. I think it was a kind of veiled apology.

I had thought that we were going to see a 4th density planet so that I could get a sense of what life on earth might be like once the transition took place but Enki must have changed his mind because he seemed rather excited to show me this world instead.

We slowed our approach and in a strange sort of all-encompassing way we were able to scan the world from every position point on the globe simultaneously. Enki was jabbering on about my first lesson on space orientation or the misunderstanding of space as he put it, but I was more fascinated in the world I was gazing upon.

Especially beautiful and compelling was a mountain range I spotted almost immediately the moment we arrived. It seemed to have a unique eco-system that was nothing like I had seen before yet somehow I completely understood how it worked right down to the intricate balance of life that was set in place by invisible forces.

Enki came along beside me and mentioned something about how beautiful this place was then compelled me to focus on the life-forms or what he called early 3rd density beings. Strangely, they looked just like modern humans, minus the three-piece suits and knee-length skirts.

I was quite captivated by all this when Enki suddenly said that it was time to leave. It felt like we had been there for years, observing all the different facets of life on this planet and I felt a great sadness at the thought of leaving. The place had grown on me, almost like I had been here before.

Then I wondered how it would be when we got back to earth. Would I have aged or would I simply place my consciousness back into my old familiar body? The illusion of time made it seem like we had been away for a very long time but I had a pretty good idea that it may have only been seconds.

CHAPTER 9: Framing up the Frameworks

When I woke up the next morning I was exhausted, which made perfect sense because how else could I feel but tired, I had just been to Mars and half- way around the galaxy for all I knew. The part that flabbergasted me however was not necessarily standing on the surface of Mars, although that was pretty cool, but how lucid and real it felt.

It was like my consciousness had been removed in whole from my body and placed inside this other super-body or dream-body. My god, if I could teach that to the regular guys down at the pub for a buck or two I would be rich.

My daughter Claire was up visiting for the weekend and as usual we shared dreams to try and help each other understand what they meant. During these sessions she would interpret my crazy-ass dreams while I would offer suggestions about hers. It has always been fun to banter back and forth so as we sat there one Saturday morning having a coffee, I started by saying, "You are not going to believe the ridiculous dream I had last night".

I went on to explain the whole thing in detail after clarifying who Enki was……

Claire responded as if unimpressed so I needed to kick it up a notch and fill in some background detail that would hopefully help sell the conversation. Not that I needed her to agree but I just didn't want to sound like some deranged lunatic trying to start a new religion. So I continued.

"Enki had said that the body I was in last night was more authentic to my immortal state than the temporary chemical body that I inhabit during the day. He had said that the whole world was an illusion created and held up by the internal thoughts of every individual on the planet. The earth mother herself was real, along with her co-inhabitant first density companions, wind, fire and water but everything else was a matrix of illusions.

A matrix is a complex system that is held up by a framework and Enki had said there were two such frameworks in existence on the planet. He had explained this to me while we were sitting in a crater on Mars looking out at the other planets. A rather bizarre situation I might add.

Framework 1 is what we see in our waking hours, it is what we think is the real world around us. The chair that is sat upon, tables with seemingly flat, solid surfaces, the concrete building and the ribbons of asphalt are all illusions of Framework 1.

The tall office building with an elevator is part of this Framework that makes up our world. Then there are the long tubes with wings that fly us to other places where there are other mind/body/souls doing different tasks and thinking different things.

Everything that you can touch, see, hear or smell, Enki said, results from our interaction in Framework 1. Framework 1 exists because we think it into existence and dwell in it to experience life in all of its glorious illusion.

Framework 2 however sits underneath Framework 1 and props it up. Framework 1 springs forth from Framework 2 and does not exist except for the creative thoughts of those in Framework 2. Enki said that we exist simultaneously in both Frameworks by creating the world and everything in it including the circumstances of our existence in Framework 2 while living it out in Framework 1. Although we have complete knowledge of the plans we create for ourselves in Framework 2, we act out the life we planned in Framework 1 without knowing that we designed it. We do not understand that the situations and conditions in life are designed and built by each individual to help achieve some level of growth.

Enki said that nothing happens by accident and there is no such thing as luck, good or bad. All things are planned and worked out ahead of time, calculated and agreed to by each person's inner self in Framework 2. From Framework 2 the various events materialize in Framework 1 and are acted out as planned by the persons involved. Since free will is involved, anything can happen, just like when an actor forgets his lines and has to ad-lib.

It is altogether unimaginable the amount of cooperation and calculation that occurs in Framework 2 to bring about a single event in Framework 1. And what's more unimaginable is the agreement amongst the collective inner selves of each individual involved to achieve a desired result which in some cases may be regarded as quite undesirable. And yet at the inner self level, the soul entity realizes the value of the experience even though at the chemical body level, its hell on earth.

Then to add to the complexity, there are the pre-arranged events that each individual has incorporated into his/her life that constitute the reason for being here in the first place. The major event or catalyst that brings about great learning might be the very reason for living this particular life or it may be something leading up to the reason. This can be such things as the death of someone important to you or a near-death experience yourself. Maybe it's the treachery of a friend or loved one or perhaps an accident or disease that renders one helpless.

Framework 2 sits underneath Framework 1 and is invisible to all who walk the earth even though they are taking part in running it. Do you remember the movie, The Matrix?"

"Of course I do," Claire replied. "That was one of my favorites."

 "The Warchowski brothers weren't too far off the mark with the whole concept of an illusionary world. Instead of some master programmer running a virtual reality program with authentic humans sitting in embryonic encasements providing electrical energy to a race of machines, the reality of it, if there is such a thing, is that we are the programmers. The world is still fake, but we program what happens in our lives. Sobering thoughts don't you think?"

"So you are going senile in your old age," was her reply. "You don't really believe that do you?"

"How does that saying go again?" I quipped. "A prophet is never accepted in his own town."

"Riiiight, you and your Enki; prophets in arms."

"OK, OK", I said. "But stay with me and let's see if we can make sense of it.

If what Enki is saying about our so called reality is true, the first thing I take from it is that the responsibility for everything that happens to us sits squarely on our shoulders and there is no longer a concept called blame.

The question to ask when something really bad, good, strange or otherwise happens is why I have caused this event to occur and what am I supposed to learn from it.

This question according to Enki allows the entity/person to have a sense of the concept that all things happening in Framework 1 are first designed and worked out in faithful agreement by you and your accomplices in Framework 2."

"Sure, but only if you believe the concept to begin with," Claire responded. "If I don't believe it, which I don't, then the question has no meaning for me so maybe we should go back to the original question of why we are here and why we have to endure all this pain and suffering. Certainly some more than others."

"I suppose you are right," I replied. "Let's start with pain. Pain is the catalyst that promotes growth and it's the growth that is the true focus not the pain. A good analogy to this is the use of a catalyst in a chemical reaction. The catalyst allows the reaction to proceed faster and more efficiently without actually entering into the reaction. It is the same for each situation that you may encounter in life, good or bad.

Say a really bad thing happens to you. It's not the really bad thing that's important nor does the really bad thing enter into the reaction that you have towards it. It's how you deal with the bad thing that's important. The RBT is really quite irrelevant because seconds after it happens it is no longer valid, only the lingering feelings that come about as a result of the RBT are all that matter. Just the feelings remain and these are happening inside your head. In 10 years' time those feelings will have dulled depending on the severity of the event and in 100 years they will be non-existent in any form.

So, let's pretend for the moment that a situation is created by an individual who has enlisted the support of actors and actresses all participating in the event. Enki used this example to explain how far this thinking goes.

A man is walking down the street in some city somewhere when he is encountered by a mugger who stops him at gunpoint and says "give me your dough". Enki says the situation was written in Framework 2 but because free will is at work in Framework 1, several situations can transpire as the whole scene is acted out.

Ultimately there is an opportunity for the enactment to go a 'good way' with our friend handing over the money and walking away or it might go 'sideways' in which case a gun is pushed into our friend's face, the trigger pulled and the man ceases his human existence."

"So what is Enki trying to say here?" Claire said in a 'don't give me that bullshit', manner. "Do you expect me to believe that the man wanted this to happen? Please."

"Well, yes, actually," I replied. "Enki is suggesting that the situation was worked out according to the means and desires of each entity participating in the event. The man was in the process of exiting the earth plane and was actively looking for a way to end his existence. Not in a consciously suicidal manner as this may suggest but in a deeper manner. Enki says that everyone at the inner self level knows when his/her time is up."

He had finished his business, learned his lessons and determined at this inner self level that it was time to move on to his next existence. Don't forget, death is transition, nothing more, so he seeks a way to exit the earth plane. In this particular case, he has chosen a dramatic encounter.

But since the veil is in place and free will is at work, the man may just decide to hand over his money and walk away because the outer ego is also at work here. It becomes the mugger's turn now to choose, in agreement with the terms worked out in Framework 2, how he will proceed. Since free will is still at work, he may, for his own development turn and run away with a pocket full of money. If this happens and the mugger runs away, the man gets in his car and on the way home hits an oncoming semi-trailer that has jackknifed on a patch of black ice and gets decapitated. Either way, in Framework 2 the man has decided to move on to his next existence and has determined how it will happen complete with backup plan and all. Everyone is happy."

"Everyone is happy?" Claire said incredulously. "You can't be serious?"

"Just wait, let me explain further," I went on. "The agreement that was made between the man's inner self and the mugger's inner self in Framework 2 was for the mugger to blow the man's head off. The inner selves of each of the 2 men knew that for thousands of years and for hundreds of incarnations, they were always together during their lives. Sometimes as friends and sometimes as enemies but always one providing the other with a means of exit. It was something they agreed to long long ago.

Each had a flair for the dramatic. In one incarnation, the man had run the mugger through with a sword during an ancient battle. In another, the mugger had bludgeoned the man to death with a club in a village along the Amazon.

Throughout time and history each had provided a death experience for the other and they were quite comfortable and happy with this arrangement. The agreement had been in place for thousands of years so that when the modern day event took place and the mugger actually blew the man's head off, there was a tip of the hat as the man, now a newly disembodied spirit was guided back home to debrief and get ready for his next incarnation.

This is not so hard to believe as it happens all the time in the movies. Actor 1 kills Actor 2 in a dramatic scene, then after the filming is done for the day, both men head off to the pub for a beer or two and talk about how well the scene was acted out.

This was a real example by the way, according to Enki. It wasn't a man walking down the street and being challenged by a mugger however, it was a man in a building with a sniper rifle taking aim at the other man riding in a car with his wife in Dallas, Texas."

"Wwwwhoa," Claire stammered. "Are you saying that the man was JFK? Who was the mugger?"

"Yes, the man was JFK but Enki wouldn't tell me who the sniper was because of the prime directive of non-interference since that kind of information could cause a shift in the natural course of events," I replied.

"Well that sounds a little bull-shittish, don't you think?"

"I suppose," I replied.

"OK," Claire began. "Now I have one for you. A woman is crawling out of a shack, with half of her clothes burned to her skin, all of her hair singed off and both of her babies charred to the bone and smoldering while the pilot in a jet fighter banks away after delivering napalm.

The pilot, taking his orders from his commanding officer a thousand miles away, obliterated the woman and her children and thousands like her without knowing who she was or even knowing how many others were incinerated along with her. Explain to me how the woman pre-planned that event with the pilot or the commanding officer since prior to the explosion, she had no idea of the existence of either."

"Wow that's a good one," I said weakly.

"Yes, and you also know this happened frequently during our own lifetime both in Vietnam and in Iraq," was Claire's response. "So you will forgive me if I don't buy into the concept quite yet so let's start from the beginning. How did this Framework 1 and Framework 2 thing get started? Where did it come from?"

"I asked Enki that question and he told me that he spends a good portion of his time in his dream-body or soul energy state and travels around quite a bit. I know that sounds a little funny but bear with me for a bit."

"OK, I get it, your Jehovah-buddy flies around the universe quite a bit, looking for stuff to do, go on."

"He said this was an experiment used by the powers within this dimension to allow creative intent as part of the forgetting system. In other words you create behind the veil and then experience things in front of it.

He said that the concept is well known amongst all advanced beings but the one entity that best put it into words and first explained it to humans on the earth plane was a fellow named Seth.

Enki says he knew Seth back in the days of Sumeria where he was one of the first entities to choose the new 3rd density bodies that they had fashioned. Seth had, after many subsequent incarnations on earth, chose to remain in his energetic state and has since become a great teacher around the universe.

His teachings here became known through a medium that he had had previous incarnational experiences with, a woman known as Jane Roberts. In a trance state, Jane would allow Seth to come through and speak while her husband Robert wrote down what Seth had to say about this illusion. So Framework 1 and Framework 2 were concepts explained to modern man by Seth.

"Aha," Claire said sarcastically. "I understand completely now. A ghost having a chat with Jehovah about the matrix we live in. Got it."

"Yes, well if it makes you feel any better the same idea came about from a completely different source in about the same time period around the late 60's, early 70's," I replied.

"Oh, pray tell," she said even more sarcastically.

"There was a young Hispanic fellow who was doing a post-graduate thesis at UCLA in the mid 60's. He was studying psycho-tropic plants and came across some information about an old Mexican fellow who lived just south of the border that had an encyclopedic knowledge of these types of plants and was also known to have used them on occasion.

Anyway, the young man was Carlos Castaneda and he became quite well known as a result of the books he wrote about the Mexican he had met whose name was Juan Matus or better known as don Juan.

Don Juan referred to himself as a sorcerer and a man of knowledge concerning things you or I have never heard about. The eight or ten volumes that Carlos penned contained some of the most daring and compelling concepts that I have ever come across.

Carlos would talk to don Juan and take notes while don Juan would expound upon one magnificent and confusing concept after another. Carlos never really explained what the concepts practically meant, things like "stopping the world" and "not doing", but what don Juan was essentially giving him was another look at reality. Another way to look at life but don Juan's imagery and his conceptualization was totally new and quite oblique.

Anyway, in one of the books, Carlos and don Juan are sitting in a restaurant and don Juan introduces the concept of the nagual and tonal. Carlos is baffled as to what the nagual and tonal represent. In his typical annoying, questioning manner, Carlos pesters the daylights out of don Juan to try and understand what he means by these concepts.

Don Juan asks Carlos to look around the restaurant and point to various items. Don Juan explains that he will then indicate whether they belong to the tonal or nagual. Every object that Carlos points at, according to don Juan, belongs to the tonal.

In a fit of frustration Carlos asks don Juan what then belong to the nagual. Don Juan points to a space under the table and shadows in the corner and other obtuse points of reference which are essentially empty spaces. These are the nagual, he announces ceremoniously. Unfortunately, poor Carlos is unable to grasp the concept.

But after reading the books a couple more times, it became evident to me that don Juan was indeed explaining Framework 1 and Framework 2 in his own terms."

"I might just have to read that story now as it seems fascinating that there could be collaborating evidence to support this theory of yours," Claire replied.

"It could be true, or at least as true as anything can be," I said. "I kind of look at it from a purely 'does it make sense' perspective. Does this concept explain stuff that previously has been unexplainable or are we simply rationalizing?

Now take Seth's concept of Framework 1 and Framework 2, substantiate it with don Juan's idea of the tonal and nagual then marry that to Enki's ideas of positive and negative polarity along with evolution of the mind/body/spirit. I think this provides a better explanation of the crazy, stupid, weird world that we live in better than any other concept that I have come across.

I for one find it more appealing to suggest that I am in charge of my life and I am making decisions for myself in the best interests of myself and those who are near and dear to me in an effort to evolve and improve myself and those around me."

"Whoa," Claire said. "I see your point but still there are many who find solace and comfort in other beliefs that they don't have to think too much about.

Nobody goes out and tries to understand their belief in terms of trying to explain the muddled, tangled, incomprehensible things that we hear about on the news all over the world. But even more than that, I believe there are just some things that happen that are unexplainable no matter what you believe.

For example, some guy walks into an elementary school with an automatic weapon and opens fire on teachers and children then kills himself. How can anyone, religious or otherwise hope to explain such an event especially in light of the response from the NRA.

Our bold defenders of freedom and rights suggested that had the principal and teachers been armed, they would have been able to defend the children. The only thing more absurd would have been to suggest that we arm our children as well. Why not?

How do you think your Enki would explain that one?"

"Jeez whiz," I replied instead of my usual goddamit. "I'll have to ask him that next time I see him. So here's my take.

One of my first conversations with Enki back in Vietnam right after I got over the initial shock of sitting and having a beer with the Lord was how the Annunaki had opened the door to 3rd density here on earth.

Up until then, Earth had predominantly been a 2nd density planet with first and second density life existing in some sort of balance that we typically see in the animal world today.

When the door opened as the result of Enki's genetic handiwork, earth became a new playground for existing entities who were working in 3rd density from all over the universe. Enki said that a council of advanced beings formed so that there was some order to the immigration policy, sort of speak.

Since earth was fashioned as a newly transitioned 3rd density planet it was determined that free will would co-exist with choice and the veil. Choice meaning having to choose your polarity for future advancement to 4th density and the veil meaning forgetting who you are when you enter the earth plane.

But suffice to say Enki and his cohorts caused Homo-sapien to suddenly appear out of nowhere with no evolutionary links to the cave man or what we commonly call Neanderthal man. Darwin and his modern day science adherents have not found a link to what they think is a clear evolutionary progress from ape to man. There is a big gaping hole in the procession and they haven't found it because it isn't there.

Earth history starts with the Annunaki coming here looking for gold. Enki and I had visited an early 3rd density world that had progressed naturally with no interference from the outside and what I saw was hugely different from what we see today on earth.

This is how we might have progressed had the Annunaki not messed around with our genetics. The people living in the world we visited were very tribal and had learned as they progressed out of the cave and into the fields that a unified tribe was stronger and more apt to survive.

This was instrumental in the early evolutionary development of this race and gave rise to inward focus. So survival became secondary and focus shifted to development of self through what we would call the arts and meditation. The tribal units became bigger so fewer differences were noted from tribe to tribe as all became integrated. Things like clothing became more intricate and colorful while food was more varied and sensational. Knife handles became intricately carved and pictures appeared on animal skins.

People in this world realized that integration on a whole strengthened everyone and splitting up the tribe or fracturing into many tribes only created differences which ultimately led to strife and war. This did not happen so they never experienced tribal warfare or mass genocide. Moreover, the totality and unity expressed by the mind/body/spirit entities originated from a deep sense of oneness among the people.

Perhaps the most amazing thing that I noted was that there was no observable religion as we understand the concept. The people saw themselves as a unified collective, connected with the trees, land, animals and world around them. They understood that all things were alive and they respected all life even while knowing that killing some for food was a necessary part of survival.

They recognized the first density beings for what they were and had tremendous respect for earth, air, fire and water. Even today, with all of our knowledge and understanding we still do not acknowledge the most important conscious beings on earth.

They did not acknowledge any god as having overall control or domination from some airy position above. In fact, they saw themselves as not only the essence of a created being but the creator as well and therefore logically concluded that it was the collective effort of all living beings to uphold and perpetrate creation. In other words they sensed the existence of All That Is and realized that every living being had essentially sprung from the same source. The people understood that All That Is was not a being to be worshipped or idolized since each person was already a hologram of this infinite being and so that would mean to worship oneself.

So, from what I could see, they got it right. They were a part of a great creation that was perpetrated by none other than themselves so there was no reason to worship or give adoration to anything else. The people assumed their bodies in a lucid attempt to experience things in a unique way on a unique planet fashioned by their collective creative spirit.

The people understood energy and how it infiltrated their bodies and connected all things living on the planet. They saw that the energy was borrowed and when it was time to give up their bodies the energy was given back to the planet body and their true essence was regained. Even today we struggle with why we are alive and what it is all about. There, they knew.

They knew that life in a particular chemical body was temporary and transitional. It was built that way to maximize the experiential evolutionary development needed to achieve value fulfillment. They knew their authentic energetic form was spirit in nature and immortal. Life and death situations took place every day amongst them but it was known by all that these were transitional and meaningful for their development. They understood death while we still struggle with this concept here on earth. There, death was a celebration.

Life has progressed on that planet now to the point where there are only 3 tribes worldwide and they cooperate with each other on all levels. They still live off the land as you would describe the Aboriginals in Australia before the British came or the North American Natives before the English and French came or the South American Indian before the Spaniards came.

They integrated with the land and they developed only as needed to express themselves artistically or emotionally. There wasn't the need to grab resources or to place one person's interests above the other. There was no monetary system to measure one man's accomplishments against another. All had equal access to the resources and means to achieve a meaningful existence. Men and women were equal.

When we look at our own development here on earth compared to the place I just described, we see how far humans have gone off track from the start.

I think of Enki's explanation of how the Annunaki messed with our genetics to produce an intelligent worker for the gold mines, as farfetched as that sounds, it does provide an explanation for a lot of things we see today. We see it in conjunction with an influx of other entities from other parts of the galaxy intermixing with the newly generated native species which produced a world of chaos and mayhem.

Early Homo-sapien experienced a million year shift in evolution almost overnight.

Before the change, Neanderthal man probably experienced life in small tribal units based on survival and propagation of the species not too unlike our friends in the early stages of the other world I just described. After the change, newly minted Homo sapien saw these wonderful and powerful beings amongst them with long white robes and red beards.

The gods were ready and willing to share knowledge on all things that would improve life such as agriculture and horticulture, animal husbandry and wine making. Suddenly life was not such a great struggle and there was time to learn other things of a finer nature. Work in the mines had become a regular and necessary part of life just like we go to work today.

Meanwhile, the Annunaki portrayed themselves as gods to help fuel their arrogance. Modern man is hugely arrogant and where did he get this? Easily from living amongst the gods and then inventing new gods throughout history once the Annunaki left.

It is absolutely clear to me that religion in our world began when the Annunaki left. Our ancestors saw that the gods had moved to the sky then told stories about how the gods had once lived amongst them.

At about the same time our world was opened up to other beings wanting to incarnate on this new 3rd density world and as we might expect, our world became populated with many different types of beings with many different points of view from many different parts of the universe.

Then as these differences manifested in the lives of all the beings populating the earth in combination with the incumbent Homo-sapien with their unique perspective of the gods, it's easy to see how strife was introduced. To take this one step further, it became evident that differences in world views would eventually lead to arguments, arguments would lead to skirmishes and skirmishes, as whole races lined up against each other would eventually lead to war. And it did.

There became a need for war gods and so Homo-sapien who had memories still intact of living with the gods, desperately needed gods to lead them in war and so they invented them. As one example, the Abrahamic tribes that had split off from Sumeria many centuries before had already fashioned a single god out of the pantheon of gods represented by Enki, Enlil and their families. Abraham's El Shaddam became Moses' war god, Yahweh. The Babylonians had Marduk and the list goes on.

Polarity was as unknown then as it is now, but to complete the explanation of early earth history and how our world became wrought with war and killing, the beings who were populating the earth from other areas of the universe were from negatively polarized worlds.

Enki explained to me that negatively polarized simply means to be in service to self. But interestingly, he also expounded on how a negatively polarized race organizes itself to establish order.

Negatively polarized peoples bring order in an age old fashion, by force or as some would say, by the sword. It was the only way known as it had been repeated on other worlds many times over. There is nothing wrong with the methodology as it produces results as surely as the rising sun introduces a new day.

Just think of the Spaniards and the journey of Cortes to the new world. It was to conquer then plunder until a new order was established. This scenario has been repeated time and time again throughout history.

So after that lengthy explanation it might make sense to suggest that there are those here who do not place any value on the experiential existence and seek to establish a forced order and therefore do not partake in Framework 2."

"Sounds plausible," was Claire's response. "Still, I would regard that as a bit of a stretch. But I suppose if you had children from China, Africa, England and Brazil playing on an unsupervised playground there would be cultural differences for sure.

But if the boy from Brazil grew up in the slums, the boy from Africa was a child soldier, the boy from England was the son of a drunken hooligan and the boy from China was from an elite family it might make for interesting observation. So maybe it does make sense."

"I didn't even have to argue the point," I replied. "You did it for me. So here is the bottom line, according to Enki. The cement that holds Framework 1 and Framework 2 together is the fact that we create our own reality. I've said this several times but to understand how we create our reality one must marry it to the Frameworks. Having done that, one then begins to fathom the depths of knowledge that is ready and waiting for us to explore."

"Fair enough," was Claire's reply. "So go ahead and explain the concept of 'you create your own reality' to me so that I can understand that as well."

"Alright then," I began. "Enki told me that what he learned about the inner self, ego and creating your reality came from Seth and here is what he said:

"Each of us simultaneously exist in other realities and other dimensions and the self that you call yourself is but a small portion of your entire identity. This inner self has lived many lives and adopted many personalities. You have constant contact with your inner self, but your outer ego is so focused upon physical reality that you do not hear your inner voice.

The inner ego or inner self organizes 'unconscious' material as the outer ego manipulates within the physical environment. It is this inner self, out of massive knowledge and the unlimited scope of its consciousness that forms the physical world and provides the stimuli to keep the outer ego at the job of awareness.

It is the outer ego's ignorance and arrogance that makes its view of world activity seem chaotic. The outer ego is spoon-fed, being given only those feelings and emotions that it can handle. This data is presented in a highly specialized manner, usually in terms of information picked up by the physical senses.

Now, if you realize that you create your reality through your own thoughts and desires, then you have learned the most important aspects of reality.

You create your reality according to your beliefs and expectations, therefore you should examine these carefully. If you do not like some aspect of your world, then you need to examine your own expectations. Realize that your physical experience and environment is the materialization of your beliefs.

If you find great exuberance, health, effective work, abundance, smiles on the faces of those who you meet, then take it for granted that your beliefs are beneficial. But if you find poor health, a lack of meaningful work, a lack of abundance, a world of sorrow and evil, then assume your beliefs are faulty and begin examining them.

It does not do any good to repress negative thoughts, such as fears, angers, or resentment. They should be recognized, faced and replaced.

You must watch the pictures that you paint with your imagination. Your environment and the conditions of your life at any given time are the direct result of your own inner expectations.

You make your own reality, or you do not. And if you do not, then you are everywhere a victim, and the universe must be an accidental mechanism appearing with no reason. So that the miraculous picture you have seen of your body came accidentally into creation, and out of some cosmic accident attained its miraculous complexity. And that body was formed so beautifully for no reason except to be a victim.

That is the only other alternative to forming your own reality. You cannot have a universe in between. You have a universe formed WITH a reason, or a universe formed WITHOUT a reason. And in a universe of reason, there are no victims. Everything has a reason or nothing has a reason. So, choose your side!"

"It makes perfect sense then," I went on to say. "Seth destroys both Darwinism and Catholicism with one good swipe of reason. We live in a universe of choice not chance and there is no god making decisions for us. Every one of us has a reason for being and if you don't know it, then you have just not thought about it. It is not about glorifying a made-up god nor is it about a senseless life of misery and suffering.

It means that evolution as Darwin envisioned cannot possibly exist as each and every living creature has a choice in its reality. Things don't happen by chance they happen for reasons so that chance mutations, although they occur, do not cause a progressive increase in the complexity of living things.

And by the way, most things are alive not just the things that we humans determine by such arbitrary definitions as metabolism or cellular activity. Trees are alive, rocks are alive, water, clouds, air and the earth herself are all sentient beings with purpose and awareness.

The real God, "All That Is" whom I have also been calling The One Infinite Creator doesn't care one iota whether you acknowledge, worship or offer sacrifices to him/her/it on any level because he is you and you are him."

CHAPTER 10: Mind/Body/Spirit and the Tarot

While pondering my thoughts after the lengthy conversation with Claire, I realized that perhaps another completely different world view was born and that Enki had helped to get my mind adjusted to these new concepts.

Quite frankly, I could explain most situations reasonably using my new system of belief. World events that appeared daily in the news were also easily seen and understood when gazing through this new pair of glasses.

Holy cow, I thought, realizing that I had just called it my new system of belief when I wasn't even sure I believed it to begin with.

I guess maybe it was new to me but in reality, this system of belief had been around for thousands of years. It seemed like we humans were willing to give up our own creative powers and powers of perception to hide our true nature. Then, instead of accepting responsibility for our acts of creation we made up gods to take on these powers.

 It was on a day when I was contemplating these concepts and wandering around the heart of the downtown area where the river runs through the middle of the city that again seemingly out of nowhere, Enki was sitting on one of the benches facing the water and throwing pieces of bread to the ducks.

"Hey," I said in a loud voice hoping to startle him. "Don't you know it's illegal to feed the ducks."

In typical Enki fashion, knowing I was behind him all the time, replied, "Yeah, I know, but just let them come and try to take me away."

"So you are an anarchist as well," I replied

"Not really, I just like to act tough."

"Well, I have been thinking a lot lately about what we have been talking about and have had conversations with normal people as well.....no offence, to test my sanity. I have concluded that a new system of belief has been created that actually explains things in a new and meaningful way. I am quite excited."

"Good, I'm glad but be certain, this is not new. This philosophy has been around on your planet and has been understood for 5000 years or more. I have told you that many advanced spirits have come and tried to explain this to you but you have been stubborn and slow on the uptake."

"Yes, well as a spokesman for the human race let me say that maybe we are finally getting it. At least I am."

"Again, this is good. Now let me tell you of another system of study that is available to humans that have been around for a long long time. These concepts were introduced to the Egyptians by another race of beings that no longer live here and were meant to help humans understand more fully about their own selves. It is called The Tarot."

"Isn't that a form of fortune telling? Didn't the gypsies use these cards to predict the future?"

"Yes, but that wasn't the intent and it certainly wasn't the gypsies, as you call them, that introduced the astrological aspects of the cards. It was in fact the Chaldeans or Babylonians who were the great astronomers and they were the ones that introduced the so called minor arcana to the already existing major arcana.

The portion of cards known as major arcana were the original set of figures put forth to the Egyptian priesthood in an effort to promote a deep study of self. It was part of the mystery school movement that originated in Egypt and the figures were drawn and introduced to the Egyptian priests by a society known back then as Ra.

Later, the Chaldeans added the court cards and minor arcana to the original deck. These were used for divination and the Tarot deck was born. It was this deck that was later adapted to produce your common day playing cards."

"Wait just a darn minute," I said. "I have never heard you talk of Ra before. Wasn't Ra the sun god of Egypt with Ptah as his father? Since the gods of Egypt were in fact the gods of Sumeria I believe Ptah was you, Ra was Marduk and Isis was the daughter of Ra while Osiris was his son. Am I right?"

"Well sort of," Enki replied. "The ancient writings that were handed down were written in a much different language and the literary style was quite unlike what you are used to seeing. The meaning or intent of a passage was never front and center nor was it ever written in plain terms. Meaning was always hidden in stories and myth.

The Egyptian Book of the Dead, the Emerald Tablets of Thoth and the clay fragments of Ur were written as poetic and mythological. Great powers were attributed to the gods and their very word could bring down mountains. True to an extent but mostly romanticized in its depiction.

But to answer your question, yes I was Ptah to the Egyptians, the great father of Ra who was indeed Marduk my son. Isis and Osiris were very special in Egypt and although all the other members of my family were identified with Sumer, these two were uniquely Egyptian. More about Isis and Osiris later but to speak of Ra in context of the actual beings who called themselves by this name during the time of Egypt is a whole different story.

Hmmm, where shall I begin? Do you remember when I explained to you about the densities and that when we came to the earth 6,000 years ago that we, the Annunaki were 3rd density beings and that the humanoid creatures that we discovered here were in fact 2nd density beings?

We hurried along the 2nd density folks into 3rd density with our genetic splicing and as time progressed we began to see splits in the way of thinking and mannerisms of the different tribes. Just like when Abram split away from Ur, we were seeing other factions peeling off the mainstream civilization that we had cultivated. You have to understand that I am talking terms of thousands of years.

The Egyptian culture resulted from just such a rift that happened in Eridu where a priestly sect split off to seek new freedoms.

These priests and priestesses wanted to express themselves differently than the mainline Annunaki who were more in tune with pretending to be gods. Both Enlil and I supported this effort because we saw value in having this split occur and the new possibilities that could come of it.

We were both aware that had it not been for the balance of spirit and science back on Nibiru, we may not have survived the ecological imbalance that had been thrust upon us. So we not only let it happen but encouraged it.

I went one step further and helped establish a new settlement along what you know today as the Nile River. With the priests also went a large contingent of men and women who were supportive of the movement.

So in the early days of the Egyptian dynasty there was a mix of well advanced 3rd density beings and late 2nd density or early 3rd density folk. Into this mix came Ra. I must admit, I was surprised. Imagine the great god of wisdom, Enki, surprised by the appearance of Ra.

What I failed to realize was the very nature of the priestly sector which was separated into the Osirians and Isians had caused a call to go out. The call was on a mental plane and was heard by Ra, a 5th density social memory complex.

"OK, stop", I said. "Obviously we have talked about 4th density and up until now I have not heard you say anything about 5th density and I imagine there might be others by virtue of the numbering system but 'social memory complex'? What on god's green earth is that?"

"A social memory complex," Enki explained, "is when a culture or society of beings are of like polarity and mind. This society then enters into the next density as a unified body in which cooperation and thought takes precedent over physical existence. The physical vehicle is no longer needed in 5th density hence the memory complex. In other words, these beings exist in the mental plane only and no longer need to walk or talk. They are integrated on an energetic plane and exist with a common purpose. To serve.

Remember when we talked about the chaos that exists in your present world because of the mixtures of polarity?

The harvest takes place to separate the masses into their respective polarities and promote the entire populace to the next level if they are of unified polarity. Ra was just that, a unified society of positively polarized people who had graduated to 5th density. They heeded the unified call of the 3rd density priests in Egypt."

"OK," I said. "Six months ago I might have said bullshit but you have spun crazier yarns than this one. But please do tell, where is this 5th density planet that is the home of Ra?"

"It is the planet you know as Venus."

"VENUS?"

"Yes Venus. Is there an echo in here? Venus."

"Well pardon me but isn't the temperature on the planet surface 67 million degrees Celsius and the CO_2 content of the atmosphere a gazillion parts per million?"

"Have you not been paying attention to anything I have said, my boy? We do not use the same chemical vehicle for experiencing 4th density work as you do for 3rd density so what makes you think that 5th would be the same as either 4th or 3rd? The senses are different and there is no body. They happily exist on the mental plane only.

Each successive chemical complex gets lighter and closer to spirit as you progress up through the densities. Not so hard to understand is it?"

"You will have to forgive the thick bone that seems to surround my small brain but please continue."

"So Ra heard the call and came to earth."

"So, how did they get here, spaceships?"

Enki just rolled his eyes. I thought it was a pretty good question but judging by his reaction I didn't pursue it.

"The Osirians were first to realize the presence of Ra due to their cultish practice of meditation. Ra could only be consulted when three or more priests were jointly meditating and opening up a line of communication. One would translate or 'channel' as you call it while others would translate the message. Scribes who were Isians would be in attendance to carefully script each word as spoken. Authenticity of the message was determined by the Isians.

So it was Ra who first introduced the Tarot during this time in Egypt. The cards were meant as a meditative study of human nature and the human experience. They described figures and symbols for each card and gave them names and positions. They ordered the cards to reflect the nature of mind/body/spirit which is the true make up of all 3rd density beings.

The first seven cards deal with the mind, a very powerful aspect of the human condition. For example, the first card was called The Magician and it fell into the position of Matrix of the Mind. This means in very simplistic terms that the makeup of the mind is magical in nature. I gave you a glimpse of this the other day when I showed you energy patterns.

The Magician has the aspect of limitless potential that is readily available by waving a wand which is symbolic for thinking a thought. The card was symbolized using the image of Thoth as the first magician in later symbolic rendering of the cards.

Since Ra advised that the cards be read and interpreted in pairs, the next card in the mind series was The High Priestess. The High Priestess represents the Potentiator of the Mind such that everything that the mind can become as promised by The Magician only exists as potential. The Potentiator however brings those things into being and it is The High Priestess that is responsible. The High Priestess, symbolized as Isis, was meant to depict the inner self or as you would call it today the sub-conscience. It is from the limitless potential of the mind that spring forth the daily manifestations that prop up your world.

This card alludes to another reason that your world has completely gone off track and is in a state of constant chaos. The High Priestess represents the divine feminine. Your modern world for more than 2000 years has almost completely eliminated the divine feminine from your psyche.

Your religions feature male gods and your societies have been male dominated which means you have missed out on the much needed balancing energies of the female. The balancing of the gentle female energies to counteract the aggressiveness of the male energies has been a grave mistake by the people of this planet. This balancing of energies occurs both spiritually as well as mentally so that on two important levels your societies have been completely out of balance. If you are going to have religion, then at least it should be balanced.

If you could understand these two cards, then you would see a monumental shift in behavior patterns of the mind/body/spirit entities that inhabit this globe. It's all about balancing the energies, with the most important one being male/female."

"A very interesting hypothesis," I replied. "However, I don't believe we are close to that kind of understanding. Case in point, the Christians still think that The Tarot is the work of the devil and women should not speak in church. In some places women are not even allowed to show their face. As medieval as that is, religion still holds sway over the hearts and minds of many."

"Yes, and I know this better than anyone," remarked Enki. "What you call the Holy Roman Catholic Church, by the power it was given by Constantine in the mid 4th century of your timekeeping, decreed that everything in opposition to the official word of god shall be destroyed and burnt out of existence.

I have told you this before how manuscripts, ideas and inventions all went underground to avoid persecution by the church during those dark times. Here they remained until a new age dawned which started around the mid to late twentieth century. This put your evolution back 2000 years such that those of us who felt we had messed up with our early experiments and pushed you forward in spiritual evolution could breathe a sigh of relief as things seemed to even out."

"Was that a veiled apology?" I jokingly asked.

"No it wasn't so let's go to the concept called The Devil. This concept was greatly feared and misunderstood in your time.

The Devil is card number fifteen and represents the Matrix of the Spirit in the Ra system of Tarot. The next card in the series is The Tower which represents the Potentiator of the Spirit. So we have our dual card set to start our study of the spirit which is the most complex of all.

The symbolism featured in the Devil card shows a large grotesque dragon like creature with two people, one male, one female, chained to the beast. The dragon is meant to symbolize darkness out of which the spirit comes and sometimes the human-like figures are featured with cloven hooves and a goat's head. This is to suggest that we also come from the darkness as symbolized by the devil.

Typical modern day renditions of The Devil card have its meaning as an addiction or constraint. Addictions such as alcohol or tobacco are sometimes seen as the meaning of this card and the chains are symbols of this affliction with the devil himself who is featured as the offending substance. However, Ra's intent was to use the cards as a teaching tool to discover the nature of the spirit, so modern day renditions relating this card to addictions is quite off base.

In fact The Devil is Ra's symbol for origin of the spirit. Call it darkness or call it nothingness or call it infinity but don't call it evil for the spirit is immortal and is a hologram of The One Infinite Creator.

This concept of darkness as shown by the devil was to help us understand that in the beginning there was only the Creator. Then a single thought emanated from the Creator and infinity was born.

The potentiating force of that creation was light. The energy fuelling that force was love.

This is where the lightning struck tower comes in. The Tower is the second card in the series and is the potentiator of the spirit. It provides the means for the spirit to enter into the light or perhaps for light to enter into the spirit.

The meaning of this card is not so much the tower itself or the people falling from the tower which typically gets interpreted as a breaking down of things such as pride, wealth or arrogance. But the lightning itself is a sudden burst of light that ignites the spirit and allows it to begin the journey of growth and discovery out of the depths of darkness. A darkness that is otherwise known as infinity."

Tell me, where else have you heard this theme, 'in the beginning there was only darkness'.

"Genesis Chapter 1," I said meekly with a grimace thinking Enki would laugh and ridicule me.

"Bravo," replied Enki. "God as spirit moved through the darkness and then created light in order to bring forth life as read in Genesis of your bible. God in this passage is referring to the One Infinite Creator and was borrowed from Egyptian texts which were borrowed from even earlier Sumerian texts.

It should not be a surprise then that the cards further depict the spirit as the hope contained within the wonder of a starry night, the often shadowy renderings of the moon or the joy of a cloudless day full of bright sunlight symbolized by The Star, The Moon and The Sun respectively.

Now you realize how important the light of the sun becomes as a giver of life and the illuminator of our souls. This is so that we may enjoy the brilliance of our incarnational experiences and growth potential as entities seeking a way back to the creator.

Is it any wonder that the ancients worshipped the sun sensing the importance of its function and how its light was critical to life. Not that the Sun cared whether it was worshipped or not but just the acknowledgement of its role."

 "I would like to hear more about Ra and their interpretation of the Tarot as I find this fascinating," I replied.

"Well then, let's continue shall we with the card whose name is The Star.

There are the stars in the sky which causes us to contemplate the expanse of the universe. Each star represents the possibility of other worlds, other light sources, other life forms and suggests perhaps you are not alone in this massive universe. The stars literally cause you to contemplate all things possible and things far beyond your imagination.

The Star is one of the most joyful cards in the deck and when it is drawn on your behalf or when you meditate on it, you are reminded of the infinite possibilities that are poured out on your behalf. The symbolism features Isis kneeling beside the Nile, pouring out an elixir from two jugs into the river which is meant to symbolize hope and encouragement. The human situation in 3rd density has as one of its most powerful concepts, hope.

There are an infinite number of stars in the sky on a clear night that helps you realize that you are but a needle in an infinite universe full of straw. You are part of an infinite number of entities experiencing life in an infinite number of ways."

"Gee Whiz, Enki," I said instead of my usual holy shit. "I'm feeling kind of small right now."

"And so you should," he replied. "You are small but that's where the concept of The Star best shines as you contemplate the vastness of the universe and the importance of your part in it.

Next we have the light of the moon which is completely different than the sun or the stars. It is a reflected light that can be bright when the moon is full or almost non-existent when it is but a crescent.

The concept here is likened to a walk in the forest in the middle of the night with the full moon shining bright. It doesn't illuminate everything like the sun during the day but casts deep dark shadows that play tricks on your eyes.

It draws your attention to things that may be lurking in the shadows and brings to the forefront your fears. Fear of the unknown is what the moon is all about. You are not supposed to know all there is to know or understand all there is to understand. Only All That Is knows all there is to know. The moon reminds you that your journey is fraught with doubt and mistrust and misdirection and fear. The moon is a great ally as it causes you to step back and search the shadows for meaning.

Symbols on the card show a path leading off into the mountains through a sort of gateway with the full moon shining bright. On either side of the gate are stationed wolves who are howling at the moon. It gives one the sense of mystery and intrigue and allows the student to contemplate the future even though it is ever mutable. The wolves impart a feeling of danger to be added to the mix plus there is an inkling of the intertwining destinies of 2nd and 3rd density beings

If this card was picked on your behalf or if you were to meditate on this card you would sense that something mysterious or unanticipated is about to enter into your life.

There is a lot more to share but it becomes overwhelming after a bit, especially when dealing with questionable attention spans and limited mental uptake that humans normally exhibit."

"Hey, who you callin stupid," I interjected. "I've been called worse by lesser mortals than yourself, I'll have you know."

Chapter 11: A Cordial Visit

Then one day I was working out in the yard and taking a break from all this crazy Enki stuff when a big white van pulled up alongside the street and a man and young girl got out. I watched them to get a sense of what I thought would be a religious visit from one of those silly evangelical groups who like to come by now and then to ask if we have thought about God lately. I was right, as the two walked up my driveway with happy smiles and freshly pressed clothes.

The fellow was middle aged and the girl was in her late teens or early twenties and quite possibly the man's daughter. After the introductions and a very nice opening salutation incorporating the present weather conditions the man got right to the point of his visit. He was to tell me that the answers to all the craziness in the world today could be found on a website and that website was completely free for viewing.

After correcting the fine fellow with the fact that most websites were free for viewing I asked him what these answers were about? The man asked what my question was so that he could formulate a satisfactory answer which would hopefully appease my feigned puzzlement. Although this seemed backwards, it was obvious the good fellow was evangelizing and if he could speak intelligently about world affairs and offer logically compelling, religiously based arguments to satisfy my question, I would come over to his way of thinking.

It always amazed me how folks could just drive up to your house and assume that you did not believe in God or if you did, then it wasn't the right way to believe in Him. I wondered how many people actually said, "Wow that sounds great. Where do I sign and when can I start coming to your church."

I did believe in God, but Enki was causing me to adjust that belief and it was making damn good sense. It turns out that maybe God was Enki's 'All That Is' and not Yahweh of the Old Testament. I wondered if this fellow would convince me otherwise. I was trying to be open-minded.

So I played the game and asked my question, "Why is the Middle East in such a mess and why in particular was ISIL killing innocent people and beheading journalists? What was God's plan here?"

The good fellow replied with great confidence, the usual and possibly only religiously based answer available for this situation, "It was clearly the work of Satan," he said.

"Of course," I replied. "It's a darn good thing that we have Satan to blame this on otherwise we would be lost for an answer."

If Enki was correct about The One Infinite Creator such that good and evil were balanced concepts particular to our dualistic world only, then there could be no personification of evil.

Maybe deities of the ancient world, like Jehovah, fit the needs of the people at the time and evolved as they did throughout history. The reason that Jehovah exists today is that the Jews are still around today. Enlil and Enki are no longer worshiped as gods because they died out with the Sumerians 4000 years ago as did Marduk and the Babylonians and Zeus and the Romans. Well maybe Enki was still here.

The only way it made sense to believe in Yahweh was to acknowledge the existence of Satan. It was impossible to have one without the other.

I didn't think it would fit well into the conversation if I told the man standing in front of me that I was talking with Enki (AKA The Lord God) on the merits of human experience and that I had met him in a bar in Vietnam.

The man, however, was clearly out of his element and started to fumble so I asked another question, one that I thought would be easier to answer because it was purely biblically based and the answers to it had been given repeatedly throughout the last 2000 years.

 I asked, "Tell me why the great Jehovah issued the order to Joshua to go into Canaan and kill every man, woman and child that lived there?"

The man replied saying, "Jehovah had given the land to the Israelites since the Canaanites were evil and practiced child sacrifice."

"Fine," I said. "But the Canaanites were there first and besides, Jehovah could have done a hundred different things prior to the arrival of Joshua's troops to make them go away. He could have caused a drought or a pestilence to come upon the land (methods that the Lord had already used on Egypt) or he could have found another place for the Canaanites to settle that wasn't already inhabited, like Saskatchewan. Or he could have made the land inhospitable until the Israelites got there. Then he could have made it flow with milk and honey. There are so many things that a god can do.

As for the evil nature of the Canaanites and their propensity to offer up children to appease their gods, didn't Yahweh instruct Abraham to plunge a knife into Isaac's chest? At the last moment the good Lord called it off but the idea was there. Child sacrifice was front and center in the Lord's mind. It was contemplated as a matter of obedience but there are other ways to test obedience, don't you think?"

At this point my poor friend got flustered and apologized for disturbing me from my work on that fine sunny afternoon. He started to leave and then it occurred to me that I had come up with the answer to my original question.

"Wait," I said. "The answer to my question is that ISIL believes that Allah has given them Syria and Iraq to set up a caliphate. They were given the area in the same way that Jehovah gave the land of Canaan to the Israelites. As instructed by Yahweh himself, Joshua did as he was told and so too is Abu Bakr al-Baghdadi doing the will of Allah.

Both are examples of the commander of an army carrying out orders from his God during a time of the development of a new tribe. These are identical situations with but a couple of thousand years' difference in time."

"So," I said to my now shaken friend. "You believe that 3000 years ago Jehovah ordered the mass killing of an ancient society so that the young tribe of Israel could live temptation free in a land flowing with milk and honey. You teach children in Sunday school and adults in bible study that Yahweh was justified and had good reasons for ordering the death of the Canaanites.

But I bet that no one in North America today teaches their children that ISIL has been given Syria by Allah and that Allah is justified in ordering the mass genocide of Syrians and Iraqis in order to cleanse the area so that a new society can develop temptation free."

The man began to stammer but I was on a roll and so continued, "Ordering the death of the Canaanites is not cool and cannot be justified in any way. It wasn't Satan that ordered the death of women and children in Canaan nor is it Satan ordering the death of villagers in northern Iraq? Do you honestly still believe that Satan is behind the massacre in Syria?"

"Yes, of course I do", replied the man which was the only answer he could give.

At that point I knew I had him so I went in for the kill, sort of speak.

"Well then", I countered. "Since Satan is behind the deaths in Syria and Jehovah was responsible for the deaths in Canaan that pretty much puts them both on a level playing field. How can you possibly define two examples of genocide as one being good while the other is evil? What am I missing?"

The man looked at me with a blank stare and slightly glazed eyes. The young girl must have thought that possibly I was Satan so I continued along the line of reasoning that I started with.

"No one can deny," I stated innocently, that Pope Innocent III ordered the killing of 200,000 Cathars in southern France around the turn of the first millennia. It's in the history books so why did he issue the death warrant?

I'll answer that for you. The Cathars had a different belief about Christ's authority on earth and there was that thing about the grail which true or not, seemed to scare the crap out of the Holy Roman Catholic Church. So how did The Pope justify this massacre? I am not sure but maybe he read the book of Joshua."

"That's ridiculous," replied the man who seemed to regain some vigour. "The Pope did no such thing and even if he did, he would have had good reason."

Not willing to get dragged into a discussion on what was a verified historical event with someone who was clearly unaware, I went on a new tact.

"Was Hitler justified in killing 6 million Jews?" I asked. "Was Stalin justified in killing 20 million Soviets? Was Pol Pot justified in killing countless Cambodians? No they weren't justified in any way for any reason no matter how evil or innocent those people may have been. So why was it OK for Jehovah to order the mass genocide of the Canaanites?

You see killing is wrong and everyone knows this. Mass killing is terribly wrong but if you are Yahweh then it's OK? I say no, it's not OK regardless of whether you are the great Jehovah, the Pope or Genghis Khan.

 You and everyone like you have to come to the realization that as long as you can rationalize and condone the actions of Jehovah in the Old Testament then you have no right to condemn ISIL and their actions in Syria."

Then I thought to myself that we will probably never be able to sit down and hash these differences out as long as there are ancient myths floating around about gods.

The man started to leave as it appeared as if he had had enough of my blasphemy.

I wondered aloud if the stories of violence in the Old Testament were indeed being repeated again today. It is said that history repeats itself. This may be true if in fact they were historical in the first place. But if they were myth, then maybe there was truly something to be learned.

If people started to realize this, then maybe the craziness and violence would subside. Not overnight but over time. It is only the realization that the modern world with its modern killing methods is getting more efficient at removing people from the gene pool and it is the counter action of intelligent thought and wilful intent towards a new paradigm that will get us past this nasty phase of earth history.

Enki's concept of the One Infinite Creator made sense but I don't think I was able to get that across to the man and his companion as they had already gotten into the van and sped off. I imagined a big red X being placed over the position of my house on Google Maps to warn others not to come here anymore. I was sure to have a discussion with Enki about this and find out what his perspective was on the whole Canaanite thing.

Chance meetings with evangelical folks always left me with a sense of mental imbalance, just like the Christian lady in the park.

On one hand I was talking with a fellow who convincingly shared a new paradigm of thought which made enough sense that I felt compelled to consider the madness that it represented.

Enki was entertaining, invigorating, engaging, enlightening and charismatic. So was Jim Jones which unfortunately was detrimental to the lives of those who associated with him. I had to keep things in perspective.

When I thought about the things Enki was saying I would naturally discount them straight out but then upon further reflection, I would shake my head and ponder how these things could make so much sense.

Then I would listen to people expound upon the accepted beliefs of modern man and they seemed just as crazy, like the guy that thought Satan was responsible for the crisis in the Middle East.

You would have to be absolutely mad to believe that some guy was nailed to a tree and bled to death so that somehow I would live forever. Yet in modern times these were the very beliefs that made you normal. It was a Catch 22. If you could show that you were crazy you didn't have to fly bombers in World War Two but you had to be crazy to fly the bombers to begin with, as Joseph Heller explained.

So who was the whack-job? Was it Enki for cooking up the far-out stories about ancient astronauts and genetic engineering, or all the priests and pastors who talk about how we have been condemned for someone eating an apple?

The fact that we believe everyone has sinned because some guy ate some fruit a couple thousand years ago does seem far-fetched. The solution to the problem was to send a fellow many years later to die a horrible death so that we would not be condemned anymore for the apple thing. Maybe if Adam had eaten a pomegranate instead of the apple we'd have been better off.

Jesus, after dying, then promised to come back one day, drifting down in the clouds so that all his believers could rise up to meet him. But there was a catch. To believe it you had to be crazy, but this was regarded as normal.

So, should I believe Enki who talks about The One Infinite Creator who lives inside of his creation or Jesus who talks about his father in heaven, an ancient war god from Israel, who lives outside of his creation?

Enki says that Jesus was referring to the One Infinite Creator when he talked about his father, not the Jewish God Jehovah. So if this was true, did the other things Jesus said make sense in this context?

I had to let this one percolate in my brain for awhile.

Chapter 12: What about those Canaanites?

"Enki, please do tell," I started. "You were around during those ancient times that we read about in the bible, so what about those darn Canaanites? Were they wiped out by the Israelites as depicted in the Book of Joshua?"

Enki smiled as if he wanted to pat me on the head and say there there, let's not get silly now. But true to form, he was not patronizing in the least and the smile was one of sarcasm stemming from knowledge.

"You see," Enki began. "By the time these events took place in the land of Canaan, Enlil had pretty much taken up the mantle of Yahweh and I had bowed out. The Israelites were Enlil's people and he gave the commands.

No, the Canaanites were not wiped out by Joshua and his troops. In fact, they entered the land of Canaan and settled peacefully in and amongst the incumbent peoples.

As time went on and relationships were established there became a mixing of gods such that the Canaanites and Israelites shared ideas and theology. Some of your archaeologists are finding evidence of this intermixing now.

It was much later during a period in the bible known as Kings and Chronicles that the Israelite nation, through its leaders and scholars, forged its final theology of monotheism. It was during this later time that it was written in the Bible that Yahweh issued the command to kill the Canaanites.

Quite the opposite was true because in reality the god of the Canaanites was El and the god of the Israelites was Elohim, the Hebrew translation for God. El being a linguistic shortened form for Elohim was in fact the same entity. Just like my name was Ea to the Akkadians and Enki to the Sumerians which are merely linguistic forms of the same name.

The original ideas of Abraham were rekindled and the pantheon of gods became one and El/Elohim was forged into an all-powerful god; Yahweh, issuing orders of damnation and destruction. No Canaanites were killed. In behind all this was of course, Enlil who spoke to Abraham and Moses directly and then later through the so-called prophets."

"Very interesting," I said. "It's like all these stories about the great Yahweh speak to an evolution of thought and invention.

 "That's correct," Enki replied. "You have god depicted in the first chapter of Genesis as spirit moving across the dark empty spaces and choosing to create. This in fact was borrowed from the original writings that we brought to Earth with us describing The One Infinite Creator and the beginnings of the universe.

Next, you have a description of Yahweh walking through the Garden of Eden looking for and calling out to Adam and Eve as if he were human. This again was borrowed from our writings and in this case it was Enlil looking for Adapa and Tiamet in the compound we called E.Din. He knew something was up and suspected that I was behind it.

Later, Yahweh became a synthesis of Enlil and I as Abraham tried to understand what he had seen and experienced as a unified albeit confused theology. After that, as the memory of Abraham faded and the banner was passed on to Moses the theology changed.

Don't forget, Moses was exposed to all that was in Egypt at the time including its mystery schools and teachings. Then when I bowed out and Enlil took up the mantle of Yahweh, this brought forth the vengeful, rule laden god that appears in Numbers and Deuteronomy. Enlil was such a jerk.

Meanwhile Moses had a falling out with Pharaoh at that time and since he was writing down the history of the Israelites he chose to make his people the victims of abusive slave masters. This was never the case.

After Moses passed on and the young tribe settled in the land of Canaan peacefully, Enlil and I and the rest of the Annunaki took leave of earth and went back to our home planet. This allowed the Israelites, over time, to fashion their god based on the attributes of not only Enlil's pissy demeanour but also my loving, gracious disposition."

"That sounds a little self-serving don't you think," I interceded.

Yes, well the kings of Israel took it upon themselves to bring god back to a unified idea. They rewrote the story to what is currently seen in the Old Testament to reflect the monotheistic theology of King Jeroboam. What you also see intertwined in the prose are the writings of the Annunaki and Sumerians which are repeated in the Babylonian and Akkadian myths.

But there is something really funny that I want to share with you. Do you remember the story in Exodus where Moses led the Israelites out of Egypt and was trying to establish rules for the young tribe?"

"Sure, that's where Moses went up the mountain and there was thunder and a great cloud of smoke while he met with Yahweh which I presume was Enlil. I assume they pontificated upon things, kind of like you and me in Vietnam. Then a couple days later he came down from the mountain with the so-called 10 commandments."

"Right you are but it was me at the top of the mountain having a chat with Moses not Enlil. The thunder and smoke was actually coming from my ship which I had put in park instead of turning off.

I chuckle about this even today when I read that passage in your bible about when Moses asks my name. I replied, 'Eyah asher Eyah' which means 'I am Eyah'. That is the way my Akkadian name, Ea is pronounced, Eyah. But your modern day bible translates this as I am who I am. Hilarious, don't you think. Poor ol' Moses thought I was the great Yahweh when really it was Enlil who was supposed to be Yahweh. Moses was a pretty good guy though and I liked him.

Now here comes the really funny part. I knew the Israelites believed that Yahweh's ancient symbol was the bull since the bull was in fact Enlil's sign. Enlil had made that infinitely clear to them in his usual pompous way.

I could also see that at the base of the mountain, the people were fashioning a golden bull in celebration of Moses meeting with Yahweh (Enlil) so I thought it would be a pretty good joke to tell Moses that I no longer wished to be symbolized by the bull and from now on there would be no symbol or graven image at all. I knew this would really piss off Enlil when he found out.

Moses went down the mountain and became infuriated when he saw the golden bull. Man, did I have a good laugh. Poor Moses, he fell pretty hard for that one. I had to make him up a new set of commandments.

I felt bad later as Enlil became enraged when he found out what had happened. He did not allow Moses to cross the Jordan with the rest of the tribe and the reins were instead passed on to Joshua. My brother was such a douche as you would say and couldn't take a joke."

"For me, that was one of the great mysteries of the OT," I said. "I just simply could never understand why the Lord was so pissed at Moses but did you really give him the 10 commandments and then tell him the cock and bull story about the bull. I was always puzzled why Moses got so mad when he came down from the mountain. You put him up to it as a joke?"

"Sure, why not? What else was there to do except get the better of Enlil. He was always so serious about that kind of stuff."

"OK, but wasn't your symbol that of the snake which today is also a symbol for the Devil?"

"Very true," was Enki's reply. "And that is exactly what I want to talk to you about today. The concept you brought up when you engaged the gentleman last week in conversation. The idea of Satan or the Devil."

"Right, but how did you know about that conversation, you weren't there."

"Wasn't I?" Enki replied with a smirk. "As in our dreaming bodies we can do many interesting things, so too can we join in, from afar, on a conversation. The importance of the concept of Satan attracted me to the conversation, so I attended. Hope you don't mind."

 "Nope, not at all," I said. "But what's the big deal about Satan? To me this is a cop-out concept used to explain things that cannot be explained by a good and loving god alone. It speaks to duality and in this case a duality that is evil personified."

"You are on the right track as far as common knowledge goes," Enki replied. "The concept of The Devil is used as an embodiment of evil to help explain how things go wrong in a world supposedly created by Yahweh.

We talked previously about an alternate idea of two well-defined paths back to the Creator, one that features self-serving behaviour and one that is selfless. Here there is no need to create beings that symbolize the essence of good and evil. It more defines how the experience of interaction comes about.

But there is one last point I would like to make concerning the Devil before I take my leave for the day. In the so-called Garden of Eden as portrayed in your bible, it was the devil described as a snake that convinced Tiamet to take a bite of the apple and to persuade Adapa to do the same. My ancient symbol was that of the snake so it shouldn't surprise you that the biblical story describes me suggesting to Eve that eating the apple will bring about a greater transition, self-knowledge and civilized behaviour.

Most civilizations do not condone people running around naked, in fact quite the opposite. Civilizations are built upon civilized behaviour and this was the first lesson I was trying to teach to my new creation. That is why when my brother came along and noticed that Adam and Eve were clothed, he had a pretty good idea that I was behind it all.

So in his usual obstinate way, Enlil condemned Adam and Eve then drove them out of E.Din, and set the barriers in place so they could not return.

Yes, I was pissed and it wasn't the first time that Enlil and I had crossed swords but I had to respect his position as Lord of the Earth. I was Lord of the waters so it was out of my jurisdiction. Maybe now you have a better idea of why I played the joke on Moses. It was just to take a shot at my brother."

Chapter 13: The End Times

"So tell me Enki, why all the craziness in the world today," I began. "I had the conversation last week with that silly religious man about why we have all these wars, senseless murders, unrestricted greed and natural disasters. His explanation of Satan being at the core was somewhat disappointing to say the least. Maybe there have been periods of earth history where conditions have been similar or worse, but from my perspective, at least from what I know of history, what we are seeing today is unprecedented.

I know that in 1666 the year of the great fire in London as well as the demise of 100,000 people due to the plague it must have seemed like the end was near. Especially since the last three numbers in that year might be related to the beast in Revelations as described by the number 666. But these were isolated events in one localized area whereas what we are seeing today is worldwide.

Granted there are more people alive today than at any other time in history so when there is a natural disaster like the Tsunami of 2004, more people are killed than ever before.

When a terrorist attack happens, there are more people concentrated in areas which translate into more deaths. Plus because of Facebook and Twitter, everyone knows instantly that a disaster or attack has happened regardless of where it took place in the world.

Is there any kind of meaning to this craziness?"

"Yes, of course there is," Enki began. "We are in the end times as all of your ancient literature suggests. You don't understand the timing of the events because you don't understand time.

So let me start by telling you that time as you know it is distorted. Not on purpose but from a misconception of your scientific community and your so-called modern thought process. You see time as being linear like a railroad track that has start point and an end point.

Time, however, is not linear; it is circular and simultaneous with no start or end. But since time is an illusion you will never understand it completely until you transition beyond the veil.

Therefore, let me say that time in third density is like a river. Your understanding of time would suggest that there is a single bridge over the river and you are in a car that travels from one side to the other and then continues down a long straight road.

I would suggest that time is more like you are in a boat crossing the river. You may choose to go straight across or you may go upstream or downstream before crossing to the other side.

Each time you go upstream or downstream the landscape changes as you cross to the other side. This is more like how the layering of time works in your present world. The river is the flow of time and the changing landscape on either side of the river represents specific periods separated by the river of time.

 You can go forward or backwards in time or visit different periods as easily as you go up or down a slow moving river in a jet boat. Every one of you has this ability; however, since you do not think that it is possible, it therefore becomes impossible.

What I am trying to say is that time is simultaneous with all earth history still being enacted on all levels. That is why your bleed through dreams speak of co-existent experiences from different time periods.

You may be in several time periods at once. You could be a soldier in Napoleon's army, an African tribesman, Viking, monk or rabbi at any period throughout earth history all at the same time. Why not? You are here to experience as much as you can so why wouldn't you give yourself these opportunities all at once?"

"How can that be Enki," I replied. "It is so different from our understanding of time that your concept is hard to absorb."

"Look at it this way then," Enki said. "If the earth was a flat disk tilted directly towards the sun with one side always facing it so that there was no differentiation of seasons nor day or night, then it would seem to always be daytime in the summer. You would go to bed in the daylight and wake up in the daylight. One of your primary means of measuring time, the 24-hour clock, would cease to exist because the earth would always face the sun and it would always be daytime.

Think about it. A simple mental exercise of changing the physical nature of the planet and its orbit around the sun takes away the appearance of time.

You gear everything on the daily rotation of the earth which is broken down into minutes and seconds. The bigger fractionation occurs when you break down the orbit of your planet around the sun into years, months and weeks.

In all realities, there is no such thing as time. There is the appearance of time but time itself does not exist. What does exist is the ever present now. All earth history is still going on in each and every time period."

"This is hard to comprehend Enki," I replied. "I can read about earth history from thousands of years previous to today. Even if the history books are wrong about a lot of things, I am still pretty certain that the descriptions given weren't all fabrications and that one event led to another which presupposes a linear timeframe.

It would seem likely that the Assyrians were warlike conquerors followed many years later by the Romans followed by the British then followed by the Americans. All in linear fashion.

There was overlap but each existed at different times in the past and quite frankly one flowed into the other as I understand it. I am not alone either since there are a whole bunch of really smart people called Historians and Archaeologists who are in agreement with this concept. Am I right?"

"No, you are not, as usual," Enki replied. "The past, or history as you know it, is but a memory, a chemical interplay of electrical impulses inside your skull which you and all the other smart people in your world call the brain.

As you know, this can be changed and manipulated. I could go into your brain right now and wipe the slate clean with an electrical current. I could even rearrange the nerve ending of your brain to produce a new memory. And if I can do this to you, I can do it to anyone. This has already been done in your scientific experiments.

So what that means is that memory is completely independent of the actual events themselves.

I'm sure you have also heard of cases where traumatic accidents have wiped clean the memory of some of your fellow humans. So really, history as you know it, is stored in your brain and can be erased or changed. If this is the case, then is history real?

Experience is experience and completely independent of memory. Storing experience in some electro-chemical jumble of grey matter inside a thick piece of bone does not confirm the existence of time.

Extra thick in your case."

"Hey what are you trying to say."

"Well, rather than remembering a pleasurable experience, wouldn't you rather experience it again and again in the now? Rather than be horrified by unpleasant experiences wouldn't you rather wipe them clean as if they didn't happen? Human experience is not stored in the brain but outside of it. Some of your adepts in the past have called this the ether.

History is ever changing and it is what it needs to be.

But for the most part you are correct. The Romans existed as did the Greeks and Assyrians. And they still exist as do you at this moment. Time is so poorly understood in your so called scientific age that it makes me laugh.

Let me give you a glimpse of what time is and how it works. The Romans are still enduring the rise and fall of an empire, the Greeks are still philosophising and the Assyrians are still conquering."

"Yes, but does not one flow into the other?" I interrupted.

"No. Each era has its own existence and when an era is finished, rather than flowing into the next, it bends back upon itself. I will grant you however the appearance of flow, one into another is there but this is an illusion."

"OK Enki, I am ready to call bullshit, god or not. Let me see if I understand what you mean. You are trying to say that when the Roman Empire waned and then Europe fell into what was called the "dark ages", this was not one leading into the other, nor one causing the other but simply two separate eras?"

"Correct, finally you are starting to get it," Enki said. "But let's call it two simultaneous eras rather than two separate ones. What marks the end of an era is usually change brought about either politically or physically.

By political I mean something that is brought about by the actions of man like the waning of the Roman Empire or the conquering of a major geographical area such as what Alexander the Great accomplished. Usually the fall of an empire begins the fold. This is when time, as you know it folds back on itself and the era starts over again.

Not as an identical replica but as something slightly new, resembling the old. The Babylonians, Assyrians and Greeks are all examples of waning empires that have begun anew. Modern examples include the British Empire which has already waned and the now diminishing American empire.

However, mind/body/spirit entities choosing to incarnate during any era can come in at the beginning of the Roman Empire or the end of the British Empire. It is a matter of choice.

Other political events that are signs of the end of an era are wars or financial upheaval which serves as symptoms of an impending fold. The actual fold or the bending back of time upon itself is almost unnoticeable. Continuance is built in.

You will note that I am using the so-called modern, scientific concept of time in this exercise to help you understand how things work in the absence of time."

"Yes, I noticed Enki, just so you know, I am listening."

"That's good because sometimes it is hard to tell.

Another way this happens is when physical earth changes happen such as cooling or warming trends that effect major populations either positively or negatively. Warming is always accompanied by an increase in population as more food is available while cooling reduces population due to its opposite effect.

Sometimes the physical event that marks the end of an age is cataclysmic but most times they are not. An ice age would be an example of a slow deadly change where decades go by as the temperatures continue to cool. Survival becomes increasingly more difficult as food supplies dwindle and heating fuel becomes scarce. Populations die off as the sheets of ice thicken and slowly crawl across the landscape causing death due to starvation and freezing.

An example of a sudden catastrophic upheaval is what happened to the species you call the dinosaur. That species came to an abrupt end when a comet impacted the earth and within days their world was plunged into a deep freeze. That is why you can still find these creatures in the area you call Russia frozen solid in the ice with tropical plants in their mouth."

"Enki, I hate to say it but you are wrong here," I carefully suggested. "The animals found in the Siberian ice were Mastodons or large elephants. These were not contemporary with the dinosaur."

"Well, I too hate to say it but I was there and you weren't," Enki replied. "All these animals coexisted but since the large reptiles were cold-blooded they tended to stay in the warmer climates around what you call the equator. The mammals wandered about everywhere including the northern regions which were tropical at that time. When the comet hit, everything went cold and almost all life froze within days. Many hundreds of years later when things began to warm-up, the reptiles who had been frozen solid in the equatorial zones thawed and then rotted away. Mammals that were frozen in the northern regions remained frozen in the ice.

But let us come back to where we are today. When you see political and physical changes happening at the same time such as financial meltdowns, waning world empires, erratic weather patterns, animal species going extinct and physical earth upheavals, you have something special happening.

What you may begin to understand is that you have a choice when it comes time to incarnate. You can decide which era to be born in and within that era you have many and varied opportunities to experience the things you need in order to grow. You can choose the beginning of an era or the end of one depending on your needs.

What I am trying to say is that if you can comprehend that there are still people being born during the time of Alexander the Great, as there are during the time of Pontius Pilate, or the great Egyptian dynasties you may begin to understand the special nature of the current era.

Each era spins out its destinies while ultimately folding back upon itself to create a new set of experiences in a slightly different way but always utilizing the same environment. The fold never repeats itself exactly, allowing for slightly different conditions that create new experiences for those wanting to participate.

Think of the movie series that is called Batman. The original series of Batman movies came out 2 decades ago by your reckoning of time and was moderately successful. Another movie producer came along a few years later and did the series over but from a different perspective. This is like what I am talking about, same Batman, same Joker but new actors.

You and your fellow humans, all 7 billion of you are here because the time is special. The fold that is coming about is not normal as I have been explaining. It is a world changer."

 "You are certainly never short on wild-ass theories," I replied. "I think I might have to consider myself ready for a rubber room if I believed you on this one. But let's say I do, just for the moment. How does one era fade out while a new one appears with no one noticing?"

"Good question," Enki replied. "When an era is coming to a close by way of catastrophic physical transition such as the onslaught of an ice age, most of the population is killed off so that only a remnant remains. The generations that follow continue to live until the memory of what life used to be like fades away. The realness of the experiences held by the ancestors is no longer important. What is important are the incomprehensible truths that are conveyed from generation to generation via myth. New discoveries are made during a new era which are just old discoveries being rediscovered. This is the folding of time and is unnoticed by those living at the time.

Do you think electricity was unknown during my time in Sumeria? Just because your scientists didn't discover electrical outlets in the ruins of Nippur doesn't mean we lived in the dark. Electricity is a rediscovery of your time.

In the case of a political change which, for example, involves the rise and fall of an empire, the changes are much more subtle and the end of the era is blurred. The folding takes place in a more subtle manner relying heavily on the veil.

With the veil in place, a pre-set memory is invoked such that people born into the end of an era or the beginning of a new era have built in memories of everything needed to perpetuate and preserve the era so that it can complete itself or bend back upon itself and start over. The folding of time has enough similarities to preserve the era and enough differences to expand the experiences.

Kings and Queens of old become the new Kings and Queens. Those reincarnating into a new cycle have the opportunity to become the same personality and perhaps correct mistakes that were made the first time around."

"Whoa. You mean that if I screwed up a particular life that I can go back into that same life and correct those mistakes. Doesn't that mess up the future and cause history to change?"

"You, my friend, have been watching too much TV. The future is malleable, it bends and flexes as needed to create the backdrop for your own personal drama. You keep forgetting that you are an immortal being of infinite capabilities. So why not go back and correct a mistake, if you want.

Now, where was I? Right, old discoveries or what you might call technologies are preserved in memory and are used as a springboard for new discoveries to take place as the fold begins anew. The industrial revolution is an example in recent history of the beginning of a new fold and the rediscovery of old knowledge.

The difference in the fold that has taken place in the last 200 years was chosen so your selection of knowledge would be recaptured in crude form. You chose heavy, dense components with which to build your civilization, like concrete and steel. You chose to manipulate those energies in a cumbersome physical fashion by forging steel in massive, energy intensive furnaces and cement in large inefficient kilns. Then large machines are required to move the heavy materials around. Very inefficient.

Yet today you still cannot match the elegance, grace and symmetry of the pyramids that were built 3000 years ago by what you think were primitive people clothed in loin-cloths. When in fact it was the 5th density entities from Venus who called themselves Ra that built the pyramids. If you had seen how the pyramids were constructed, it would have made your eyes pop out of your head.

Perhaps the biggest laugh of all is when I hear your modern explanation for how the pyramids were built. Your scientists postulate that the Egyptians barged these massive stones across the Nile and then rolled them across the sand on logs. Laughable. Then they pushed these giant blocks up ramps to stack one on top of the other. Priceless.

But I digress so let's get back to our discussion of eras. It's like a spring, my friend. The coils of a spring always circle back to the starting point of the wire but slightly askew so that the spring is an accumulation of these coils. You can put force on the spring but it always comes back to its original shape. But if the spring itself becomes the wire in a new coil forming a much larger spring, then you have the continuance of an era.

So, instead of being born in this era 1900 – 2020, you could have chosen to be a Scottish highlander in the 1700 – 1900 era during the time of English/Scottish conflicts and all the violence that went with it. Or you could have been an Aztec warrior in an altogether different era. You may actually be one right now since all these time periods are still active.

If you consider that this was a choice that you made, then maybe you have an idea why you chose the particular era that you see yourself in today? Any idea why 7 billion others chose this current era as well?"

"Given that I believe you, and I am not saying that I do," I began. "It would seem that I and 7 billion others made the same choice for the same reason. You just said a few moments ago that there is something important going to happen of great magnitude. I think you are going to tell me that we are here to experience the end of an era. Am I right?"

"For the first time today, you are partially right," Enki said emphatically. "Not just the end of an era but the end of 3rd density existance on this planet all together. This is a much bigger coil in a very big spring that is starting to fold back on a massive galactic event. You might say that the giant spring is coming to an end so that a new spring can appear.

This no longer involves petty, inconsequential earth history that I have been telling you about. This is a monumental upheaval that will usher in the next billion years of experiential existence for you, me and all life in this galaxy.

Those requiring further 3rd density experiences will now incarnate on a new planet with all the necessary memories implanted to begin a seamless transition as if they were still being born on earth choosing any era they desire. The veil will be intact.

Those transitioning to 4th density will stay here, with the slate being wiped clean. The veil is no longer needed and a new set of experiences will begin. Oh, I just about forgot, time becomes non-existent in 4th density as it should be.

This is the new spring or, going back to our other analogy, we have reached a waterfall in the course of the river and we can no longer take our boat further downstream. Something new is needed to proceed past the falls."

"Whew," I said. "So we are really in the end times. When will it happen?"

"Hah," Enki said with a smirk. "Absolutely no one knows. You have had many earth prophets make these predictions and they have all been wrong. You have had channelled spirits make predictions and they have been wrong. Do you know why?"

"Actually, I wish I did but alas I don't. Please enlighten me dear Enki," I said in as sweet a voice as I could muster. I guess I was really getting comfortable being around a god. How will we know?"

"No one knows. Everyone looks for a date and time at which these changes will take place assuming that a point in time will mark the event. This is not so. It is gradual and happens over an extended period. We are in that period, but how long it will take, again no one knows. I am now trying to explain this in your terms of time.

But can you see the signs? Earth warming, tsunamis, animal extinctions, wars and financial meltdown all point to the end of an age. It's all there."

"Yes, I see the signs," I replied. "But at some point I will be sitting here maybe talking with you in 3rd density and then in the next moment we will be in 4th density. How will this happen?"

"Correct," Enki replied. "One moment you will be in 3rd density and the next you will be in 4th. You make this transition when you die. Your body will go back to the great mother and you will exist in your true energy form with all the incumbent memories that have been gathered over the millennia. You will then begin planning for your new incarnation on earth as a 4th density mind/body/soul entity, if you are ready."

"What will this look like, Enki?" I replied.

"You will look essentially the same as you do now. Your new vehicle however will be different, not carbon based as it is now. Your utilization of food will be more efficient as the body will convert the nutrients to energy in a more complete fashion. There will be less waste.

So you will continue to eat food but once per day will be more than enough to achieve a steady output of strength and endurance. You could easily go a week without food as your new body will modulate the energy output accordingly.

Waste from the metabolic process taking place in your new 4th density body will be greatly reduced but not eliminated. Reproduction will occur in the same fashion as there will still be the opportunity for masculine and feminine choice of body."

 "Enki, before you go further, you said that the new body in 4th density will not be carbon based. If not carbon, then what will be the composition and what will that look like? How will it function?"

"Your scientists today only partially appreciate the complications of silicon chemistry. The chemistry is complex because it has a wonderful and varied relationship with the other elements. One that carbon does not enjoy. A body made from silicon is much more robust and has a different sequence of inputs and outputs. Plus, it is more receptive to energy.

The viability of your present carbon based body requires first the oxygen from the air. Lack of oxygen requires only seconds before the body becomes lifeless. Removal of water requires about 3 days before the body expires. Food depravation can take weeks so there you have the order of importance of the inputs for the viability of the carbon based body.

Silicon based is much more efficient. First of all, there is no longer the need for oxygen. Instead the requirement for oxygen will be taken up by a direct flow of energy from the universe. This flow of energy will enter via the prana tube and will be distributed throughout the body from there."

"The prana tube?"

"Yes, this is also a part of your current carbon based body, but you have decided long ago not to use it. Your adepts, yogi's and guru's all knew about the chakras and prana tube. Chakras are still used and are important for balancing energies within your current bodies. They will be present in the new bodies as well.

But the prana tube fell out of use thousands of years ago when mankind decided the 3rd density bodies should breathe in energy via the interactive chemistries of oxygen.

A 4th density body because of the silicon make up only requires the direct energy input from the universe via the prana tube along with the chakras to balance out the energies within the new body. In other words, there will be no need to breathe."

"Won't that deprive us of our sense of smell," I said, thinking that maybe I had a smart question for a change.

"You will still enjoy the scent of a flower or a spring day, so what makes you think it has to come in via the nose?" was his reply.

I shuffled my feet and looked down at the ground.

"Your new skin will be like a multiple sensing device and odor will be taken in as part of that new sensory feature. Your water requirement will be next to nil as the new body will be able to go for months without it and your food requirement will be greatly reduced as well. The preparation and ingestion of food in 4th density is more a symbol of service than it is sustenance.

There will be no need for disease anymore as the new body will be built for longitivity. Fourth density bodies will last for about 10,000 of your revolutions around the sun."

"Whoa, did you say ten thousand years?" I exclaimed.

"That's right," replied Enki. "That's what I said. You see, 4th density work happens under the pretence that you know who you are. That you are complete with the memory of all your 3rd density experiences and the knowledge that you are a hologram of the Creator.

This takes you to a whole new level of experiential development requiring much longer time periods. But don't forget, time will not have the same pull on you as it had in 3rd density. The aging or lifespan of the human body was a collective choice that you all made at a level where this communication takes place. Framework 2, remember? Third density work is hard work requiring much healing inbetween lives so the lifespan was shortened.

But in 4th density, although there will be the appearance of time such as periods of day and night along with the change of seasons, your body will grow and mature till about year 35 then it will stop aging.

Therefore, the bite of time will be diminished and simply disappear into the now.

"How will death come about then," I asked inquisitively.

"Usually death will come about via a shotgun blast to the stomach."

"Really?"

"No, not really, but there is such a thing as a stupid question, besides, what does it matter? What's more important is the consciousness that you will possess in your new bodies. Since there will be no veil your psyche will be that of the inner self as there will be no need for an outer ego. You will see yourself as you truly are but now with a viable and long-lasting chemical vehicle.

There will be no confusion regarding the essence of your spirit which is embedded in the root of the mind and reflected in the body. The soul will be right up front so that the mind/body/soul will be one complete unit with knowledge of each as an integral part.

I told you earlier that 2nd density beings ready for 3rd density existence will move along with the others to dwell in a new place thus reserving earth for 4th density.

But like the co-existence of 1st, 2nd, and 3rd density beings on earth now, so too will there be a co-existence in 4th density. Those in 2nd density that are not ready for harvest into 3rd density will stay and continue to develop until they are ready.

That means that you will still have trees, animals, birds and fish to further enrich your experience as you will enrich theirs as well.

Consciousness now becomes a much more pliable tool to work with."

"What does this mean Enki," I queried. "I'm not sure I understand what you are saying."

"Consciousness in 4th density is malleable and interchangeable and is one of the main tools you will work with. Your new bodies will be fashioned in such a way as to not entrap your mind and soul as effectively as they did in 3rd density.

You will be free to explore wonderful new experiences while parking your body, shall we say. Experiences that allow you to delve into things you never thought possible."

"OK, if you're selling ice and I'm an Eskimo, I am just about ready to put down my quarter," I replied. "The 4th dimension is beginning to sound like an amiable spot to hang out, like a beach bar on a warm Caribbean night but I haven't the slightest idea of what you are talking about, even though it sounds compelling.

Perhaps an example, if you will, Enki. If of course it's not too much trouble."

"Well then, an example you will have."

Chapter 14: A lesson in Consciousness

My brain was wired to only take so much theory before I needed something concrete to get a feel for the idea. Enki was pushing me into an area that required a great deal of faith and as convincing as he was, the concept of a loose fitting consciousness was just a bit foreign.

This had been my root problem with Christianity all along. I had always been being pushed into areas that required faith when certain aspects of the theology didn't make sense. Why do good things happen to bad people and bad things happen to good people? Answers usually came about as rationalized explanations requiring a good dose of faith. God wanted it this way or that way and who can know the mind of God. This just wasn't good enough.

I wasn't in agreement with Enki's explanation either that there was no such thing as good and evil or that our understanding of good and evil was distorted. If he was right then the problem went away, if he was wrong then I was back to relying on faith.

"OK, let me start from the beginning so you can understand the twists and turns of your tortuous development since 3rd density began," Enki began.

"When we first arrived, the earth was in the throes of becoming a 3rd density planet as it was in 2nd density at that time. On its surface there was the cave man and all the birds, plants and animals. Except for us, everything was considered 2nd density beings.

We did our experiments and accelerated early mankind's evolution, then the great earth mother made her transition to 3rd density. The transition was made with some difficulty as a cleansing was needed. This took the form of a deluge and the event was recorded in almost all the ancient writings. It really happened, but not to destroy man as an annoyance to the gods, but so that the great Gaia could transition herself to 3rd density.

After the remnant of mankind was saved and life got back to normal, Ra, the 5th density beings made their debut in Egypt. So there was the interplay of 1st, 2nd, 3rd and 5th density beings all coexisting on a newly transitioned 3rd density planet.

The important thing here is that the mystery schools were established in Egypt by the 5th density beings, Ra. They taught the things that were hidden and unknown, for example, the teaching of consciousness.

Ra correctly showed the priests that man can move about in his dream body and do quite amazing things as a valid part of the human experience.

Juan Matus told you this as well since there are modern day writings describing these abilities as attributed to the shaman.

Consciousness can be transferred from the waking physical body to the dream body but this should not come as a surprise to you since we have explored that realm already."

I nodded as I remembered my out of body experience with Enki on our trip to Mars. That memory now seemed out of place as I struggled to define how that fit into my reality. It was like a dream that was cut out of some other reality and forced upon me by my own thoughts, awareness and memory. Normal dreams, no matter how vivid, always faded in memory. The experience with Enki, although dreamlike and vivid, was branded in my mind like a Hereford steer. Just as if it had happened last night.

Enki sensed I was in a self-reflective state and snapped his fingers.

"Are you back with me now?" he asked.

"Sure, carry on if you will my good man," I replied. "Can we get a beer anywhere?"

"No. So that was the first lesson given to men," Enki continued. "Ra showed that the mind and soul were viable parts that were capable, complementary and important to the human make-up. Since free will was at play, there was a varied mix of entities on the surface of the earth and a bigger struggle was at hand.

The struggle was for land and resources. Land was of great importance and the struggle to obtain it became one that propelled men towards war.

This caused the focus to switch almost entirely to the body. Mind was used to invent new ways of procuring land to support the body. Mind was also used to invent new ways to kill and eliminate the body of others so that more land could be obtained. The body became the target of the mind, while the soul was forgotten.

Pathway to the mind as a portal for development was always open and mankind had the choice at many points in history to proceed down this road but instead you always chose the body. You wanted to seek the pleasures of the body, to feed and satisfy it, to pamper it but mostly to kill it.

The ancient Greeks during the time of Plato and Aristotle were perhaps closest to the matrix of the mind but this too was lost in war. Therefore, the mind never got its proper due and technology became the rallying cry as mankind progressed into modern times.

Today you have the ability to communicate with each other but choose to have electronic devices do it for you. You have the ability to move great distances in the blink of an eye but chose slow laborious, energy intensive means instead. Your fastest jets cannot come close to the speed of a light beam when it comes to transportation. Technology will never achieve travel by light whereas the mind always could.

You have at your fingertips the most extensive database in the universe and yet you insist on using the google. You enter words into archaic search engines to seek information.

I have been to other 3rd density worlds that chose pure mind development to the point where the body was no longer needed. This was every bit a mistake as choosing exclusively, mind over body. Third density seeks balance.

So here you are, after 5,000 years of development with all of your so-called brilliant technological advances and yet so incredibly ill-prepared for the next phase of existence. That is why so many of you will not graduate during this cycle of harvest. You have become befuddled as to which path to follow and completely out of balance.

This is where mankind stands at this juncture in your evolution."

"Don't hold back or anything," I replied emphatically. "If we are so messed up or out of balance as you say, show me what it looks like to be in perfect balance. How does our state of consciousness come into it?"

"OK, let's continue with our discussion of consciousness of the human race and its evolution. I was telling you that Ra began teaching the priests in Egypt that consciousness could be readily transferred from the waking body to the dream body. Do you remember?"

"Yes, I do, please continue."

"Right, well Ra also taught that consciousness could be transferred from waking body to waking body. Here let me show you. Stand up."

We had been sitting on a park bench where Enki liked to come and feed the ducks and geese, at least until I had chastised him on the illegal practice.

I stood up as Enki had asked and was greeted with a whack between the shoulder blades reminiscent of how my adventure began a few months ago when I entered into the crazy world of energy patterns.

My head swirled and I became dizzy. I attempted to sit back down on the bench but as I proceeded to sit, my body seemed to split apart. The first part sat while the second part stood standing.

I'm sure I must have looked like a real tool standing there with an awkward plastic grin on my face and a feeling that something really weird had just happened. I looked around and saw Enki standing slightly behind me on my right with that same silly smile that he had when he had done something funny to me last time.

My body felt light so I rotated to take in the complete 360 view of what looked like the real world. That is until I spun past Enki's smiling face and got to about 270 degrees when a cold icy feeling gripped me as I froze in my tracks.

I stood looking at the park bench from about 15 feet away where Enki and I had been sitting and there we were, still sitting. I closed my eyes hoping that somehow the world would fix itself but instead I felt the same dizziness that had occurred several seconds earlier.

I was terrified to open my eyes but I knew I had to open them. Now I was back on the bench beside Enki which was good news, however, I was now looking at myself standing with Enki 15 ft in front of the bench in some sort of frozen animation. This wasn't good. It seemed I was in two places at once.

I blinked and suddenly I was standing again. My mind became numb and I began to grope at the air and flail as if I was spinning and losing equilibrium. In my floundering, I found Enki's shoulder and steadied myself.

He was looking at me and I dearly wanted to unceremoniously wipe that grin from his face but instead I blurted, "What the hell Enki, what have you done". I thought I had shouted the words but my lips didn't move. Enki heard me.

His reply came but instead of entering through my ears and travelling along the auditory nerve to be processed by my barely working brain, the words just erupted inside my head like they were already there.

"Welcome to the world of consciousness," he replied.

"Great," I replied in thought. "I'm in some crazy new world of yours, but how did you get me here. What did you do to me?"

"Nothing all that complicated," was his reply. "I altered your internal receiver so you could process a different frequency. Not too unlike tuning to a new TV channel. I just changed your channel so you could see the dimension that was already in existence but unavailable for your viewing on your previous channel. Your TV has 100 channels to choose from but you can only watch one show at a time. Right? "

"Whatever," I thought. I wasn't at all interested in how many channels I had or if the tuner was somewhere around my shoulder blade or 3 ½ inches up my ass. I only wanted to be sitting on the bench with the sun shining on my face, not in some hazy world that Enki saw fit to bring me to. Can you please change me back?"

"Don't you want to see what I have prepared for you? When did you become the chicken as they say?"

"OK, OK, but before we go further could you please explain to me how I am standing here with you in some sort of thought projection conversation while looking at myself sitting on a park bench in some sort of suspended animation. We look kind of goofy by the way."

"Yes, well you have a spark of consciousness left in your real body to keep it, shall we say, alive. You and I will sit there looking somewhat ordinary as long as no one bothers us. If someone or something comes along and disturbs us we will have to exit what I am about to show you and hustle back. The shell of our body is only capable of so much right now and with you anyway, we can't expect much more than that stupid look on your face."

Enki was right, I had a stupid look and if I had been wearing a pair of crooked sunglasses, I would have been a dead ringer for Bernie, from that movie about the dead guy."

"We both exist in a pure energy form right now that is outside the visual and audio range of most humans. In other words, we are invisible to most."

"But when I blinked and was back in my body for a moment, I could see myself standing next to you 15ft from the bench where we were sitting. What was that all about?"

"That was a ghost projection due to the split that had occurred. For a moment you were in two places at the same time and you could see from each perspective simultaneously as the rendering was taking place. Now you are here with me until we come back."

"Outstanding. Well, let's get on with it then, what would you like to show me."

"OK, then. As I was saying, Ra was teaching the priests in Ancient Egypt about the capabilities of consciousness and one of the things they taught was the transferability and transmutation of the spirit. Let me show you.

In this state we now have access to the soul or the inner being of all things. We simply ask if we may borrow a body for a while and then bring it back. All have this ability, few know about it.

I have taken the liberty to make some arrangements beforehand and so follow me to our ride."

I thought Enki had stolen a car and since we were apparently invisible, we would maybe take a corvette for a joy ride and bring it back unscratched.

"Nope, that's not it," the thought suddenly broke into my brain.

Damn, I forgot we are telepathic.

"This is our ride."

There were two sets of roller blades right in behind a pair of geese waddling down the path in front of us.

"The roller blades behind the geese," I thought.

"No, the geese," came the thought reply. "Let's go." Enki snapped his fingers.

I blinked at the snap of his fingers and the lids that opened over my eyes had a strangely thick and opaque feel. I looked and blinked again as the landscape had grown large to where it seemed I was at knee level to everyone around me.

Without time to comprehend the absurdness of suddenly being a midget, there was a rush of air and a thundering noise that arose next to my side which scared the crap out of me causing a surge of adrenaline to my muscles. I was expecting my legs to sprint me to a safe distance from the noise but instead I could feel my arms moving at a frantic pace which was quite involuntary as I certainly was not thinking that under duress I should flap my arms like a damn fool. But flap them I did.

That was the first odd feeling I had. The second was when the ground fell away and there was a gust of wind that caused an unsettled momentary unbalancing of equilibrium. It appeared as if I was airborne.

In fact, the ground was rolling beneath me and objects such as park benches and people were getting smaller, like when you look out of the window of an aircraft taking off.

The initial shock had somewhat worn off and I looked around to scope out this crazy new environment that some might call "the air" only to see a goose flying next me with a stupid shit-faced grin on its beak. I've never seen a goose up close look like that especially 100ft off the ground moving at about 45 mph.

I decided to look at my nose which I could usually see out of the corner of my eye and still yet another shock to the system was to see my metaphorical beak replaced with a real beak. This is ridiculous, I thought.

"No its not," was Enki's reply which I could hear somewhere in the back of my brain that was now apparently the size of a peeled mandarin orange. "Why should this seem strange to you after all we have done together?"

"You're right," I thought. "Why should it seem strange that I'm a freaking goose flying 200 ft off the ground." We were continuing to gain elevation and I was going to honk but that would have made the situation even more preposterous.

"Let me try to explain to you what has happened," Enki projected. "And in the meantime, keep those arms moving and follow my lead."

"OOOOOkay," I replied. Then it dawned on me that my arms weren't arms anymore but some sort of feathery appendage which I think are called wings. I still seemed to be moving them furiously up and down in a kind of flapping motion that strangely enough, if things could get stranger, wasn't the least bit tiring.

 "This is what I have been trying to tell you, consciousness is transferable. You only need agreement on the part of the participating entities, in this case the geese, in order to go flying. As you can see, that is exactly what we are doing. The two fellows whose bodies we are occupying were most accommodating."

"That's nice, so where are they right now since we are in their lice infested bodies? Are they sitting on a park bench enjoying the sun shining on their now smooth skin? Are they enjoying a nice cold beer for the first time since coming out of an egg?”

“No, it doesn’t work that way. You can only go down in densities not up.”

“Shoot, I should have known.”

 It was exhilarating to say the least. We were following the river along its course as it meandered through the city. We were flying above the street lights and power poles at a speed that my body had never experienced before.

Being in a car or airplane took away the sense of speed and freedom. That feel of pushing through the air at great speeds under your own power was indeed a rush.

“Your native or tribal societies such as the Indian and Aboriginal knew of this ability for thousands of years. The shaman, medicine man and tribal chief could perform such acts with ease. Don Juan told you about this but nobody believed him.

Your own modern society has countless cases of mysterious transformations such as witches turning into cats and shaman, shape shifting into wolves. Your scientists discount these stories as myth and legend because they cannot duplicate the phenomena in a laboratory.

If you seek out the esoteric and occult knowledge that is now available to everyone on the planet you will see that what we are doing right now has been done before by many others.

My point in showing you these things now is because it will become a normal function or a common occurrence in 4th density. Your new body will be equipped with these abilities and your mind will possess the knowledge of that ability. It will enrich your experience.

This little expedition today will give you a glimpse into the 4th density world that awaits you. But, you are not quite there yet, you still need to do work in order to sit well at the harvest. Do you get it?"

The wind was whistling in the little holes in the side of my new skull covered with feathers that used to be my normal ears. The sound of the wind in my ear pockets produced a musical tune that sounded like an instrument being played that was far far away. The undulating nature of the tune was caused by the change in pitch and yaw as I struggled to keep up with Enki's murderous pace that he had set.

I was trying to gather in the essence and joy of the experience of flying while trying to blot out all the noise coming from Enki's thoughts. He was saying something about shamans and 4th density but all I heard was blah, blah, blah.

Enki probably sensed that I was not paying attention and started to lose altitude as it appeared as if he was headed for a river landing. I estimated that we were about 10 miles from our take-off point back at the park and well out of the city.

I began to get nervous because if it was his intent to land on the river, then I wasn't sure that my muscle memory would be enough to help me through what seemed like a complicated process. After all, if I was a goose then I should know how to land, so why be nervous.

Let's see, if I slow down too much before I get close to the water I will plummet out of the air and drop like a rock into the water. But if I don't slow down enough, I'll pile drive my beak into that fast approaching gravel bar and cartwheel myself along to an inglorious stop.

I couldn't decide which was worse or which would hurt more or if a goose feels anything at all. I had watched TV shows on the Nature Channel where the cameraman had caught waterfowl making horrifically bad landings so I knew it could happen. That is if you believe everything you see on TV.

But the real question was, as a goose, would I feel embarrassed if I botched the landing? Would Enki think less of me? Surely he would take into account that this was my first outing as a goose and not judge me inappropriately. What would the sparrows, hawks and crows think? Hey guys get a load of that goose down there trying to land on the river. What a moron. But mostly I wondered if it would hurt.

As I fast approached the surface of the river with all these non-goose-like thoughts running through my head (I'm sure a goose doesn't think these things at all) my arms flapped furiously while my body seemed to come upright and perpendicular to the surface of the water. Then I seemed to know when to stop flapping my arms without knowing when to stop flapping and there was a small plop as my feathery ass settled gently into the water.

This was a mountain fed river and even in the summer it was frigid. I was expecting a likewise cold water enema but it seemed my ass or at least the borrowed ass of a goose was a well-protected part of the anatomy.

I had just touched down effortlessly and began to drift with the current all warm and cosy-like when I looked off to my right and coming up beside me was another goose which I knew was Enki.

I looked at him and laughed. "Do you realize how silly you look," I projected. "The powerful Lord God Jehovah, the incomparable Sumerian god of knowledge, Enki the Great, honk honk."

"When you are finished," Enki replied by thought. "We can get back to our conversation."

"OK, please, let's continue but forgive me if I giggle a bit along the way."

"Sure giggle all you want but don't forget, your feet are as webbed as mine. Now, did you hear anything I said while we were flying?"

"Just the middle part," I projected back.

"As I was saying, the ancients knew of this ability and even the modern aboriginals and Native Indians knew of this as well. By modern I mean the last 500 years or so.

This knowledge however is an important step in achieving 4th density harvest. It is knowledge that requires you to understand not only that you can transfer your being into another being but that all beings are vitally important ways of the Creator knowing himself.

In this world and a hundred million other worlds throughout this universe there are countless situations and actions taking place, lives lived, battles fought, births, deaths and even geese flying down the river. The Creator experiences every flap of a wing, every shedding of a tear, the joy of each birth, the running of a race, the winning or losing of a game and any other act that is universally possible.

Without attaining this knowledge in 3rd density, there cannot be a readiness for 4th density. As I said, you are ready for harvest, except for this one last lesson."

The lesson was duly noted as we flew back to the park in the central part of the city. We exchanged bodies and Enki said whatever you say to geese when you are thanking them for the use of their bodies and then I blinked and we were back on the bench.

 It was none too soon as a woman with 2 kids and a dog walked towards our bench with the potential for a hasty retreat had we still been geese. Thankfully we had given ourselves enough time for the transition to take place and had our complete wits about us as the family approached.

"Fine day," Enki said as the woman passed.

"Yes it is thank you," replied the woman as her kids flailed about and the dog sniffed my boots. I must have stepped in goose shit somewhere along the way.

"This is your birthright as an infinite being," Enki continued. "It is also your pathway into 4th density so you see the importance of what I am trying to show you."

I had been trying to decide on an intellectual level whether Enki was a lunatic or not. I even tried on a rational level to use Enki's arguments as an explanation for a world that had gone mad. Everything he said seemed to make sense and on top of that, my wife had not institutionalized me, yet.

What remained however, was visible tangible proof that Enki was a god or at least, in modern terms, an advanced soul with special powers. It seemed easier these days to have a conversation about Superman and the Hulk than it did about Zeus, Marduk or Enlil. Thank you Stan Lee.

But how the hell did he do that thing with the goose? I could deal with a trip to Mars as being a very lucid dream because everybody dreams. To take my waking consciousness and transfer it into some feathery creature that happened to be waddling by was something completely different.

Maybe it was something like how they get orange flavouring into Finlandia vodka but however he did it, he did do it.

Now I had to pay attention to the fact that I was still regarded by friends and family as a normal, sane person. If I were to sit around the supper table one night and casually tell my wife and kids about being turned into a goose the sense that I was normal might evaporate.

Enki must have had special powers to change me into a goose so I was faced with the reality that Enki just might be who he says he is.

What if someone came up and introduced themself as Jesus Christ and in a conversational manner went on to explain the meaning of life. How on earth could anyone take such a conversation seriously? Yet, this is where I found myself in regards to Enki.

I considered myself open-minded, rational and unaffiliated with any religion. I believed in God but I wasn't sure which god that meant. For the time being it seemed I was a patron of the church of Enki. As far as I could tell, there was a congregation of one.

I did not know of anyone else who could make me honk or perform a flawless landing on a fast moving mountain river.

Then without actually saying it out loud, just in case someone from the psych ward was nearby, I had to admit that Enki was who he said he was. If not a Sumerian god, then someone really special. Hmmmm.

Chapter 15: Distortions

"You see," Enki began as we sat on our usual park bench on a sunny Saturday afternoon. "Your history since the time the Annunaki first came to this planet has been confused and convoluted. There have been many entities from many worlds that have come here for many different reasons.

Ours was simple, we wanted gold. Others came later, after we left, wanting to dominate and control while still others wanted to teach and learn. The thing that made this planet desirable to so many entities was the veil. The forgetting veil was an experiment that went completely right. It enhanced and accelerated the spiritual evolution for positive and negative beings alike and therefore attracted both. This planet became the California of the Universe and everyone wanted to come here, even the entity known as Arnold Schwarzenegger.

For those who sought to dominate and control this planet for their own desires, the institution of religion was invented. When we first arrived here and naively portrayed ourselves as gods, it served our immediate interests in obtaining the natural resources that your earth provided. Plus it was fun. Homo sapien honoured and praised us and if that wasn't a rush.

Others who were negatively polarized came later and saw what we had accomplished. They used our early success in portraying ourselves as gods to accomplish their needs as well. We had unknowingly provided the template that they would use to become dominant in your world.

The concept of religion was used by the others to help control the thoughts of the earth people after we had left. The concept of religion was put forth as a way to explain the meaning of life but it was, of course, a distortion.

God loves you and wants you to be in heaven with him and all you have to do is believe in his son Jesus Christ. The message was simple and compelling but highly distorted. As I looked on from afar I thought that there was no need for action, to step in as they say, since the concept was so incredibly disjointed. I was sure no one would fall for it but Homo sapien took it hook, line and sinker to use one of your clichés.

One such religion by itself could not achieve the results of a subdued and suppressed planet so several religions were given to you and many prophets rose to prominence appealing to many different people. But in order to hide the intentions of those truly in charge, the religions had to be formed in such a way that they would be antagonistic towards each other and have competing theologies.

This truly brilliant manoeuvre then allowed for unrest, violence and war to keep everyone unbalanced. One religion pitted against another designed by the same beings to divert attention and keep you all preoccupied with your differences. Masterful.

The main idea behind the distortion of religion however was to make you think that you are inferior so that you are always looking somewhere else for the answers. The answers that some god possessed.

The fall from grace myth in the Garden of Eden and the saviour myth were designed to impart a feeling of need. The idea was to suggest that humans were flawed and broken in the eyes of a powerful being that lived in the sky. This was followed many centuries later by providing a solution to the problem by offering a human sacrifice to atone for your sins (to put it in those religious terms) and thereby achieve forgiveness. Did it ever occur to you that there is nothing wrong with you to begin with? Let me take that back, the only thing wrong with you is that you are gullible.

The place called E.Din did exist as did Adapa and Tiamet. If there was a lesson to be learned from the Garden of Eden, it was that Enlil was a jerk.

Sometimes history can be so simple.

The famous heads that are situated on the island that you call Easter Island, gazing to the heavens, were designed by the same negative beings to suggest that there are gods up there. The stone heads gave a sense of where the gods lived and perhaps that they would return one day from above.

Your historians have noted from the clay tablets of Sumeria that our time on earth was the only time in earth history in which the gods lived amongst the people. It was true. We portrayed ourselves as gods and lived amongst the earth people whom we had fashioned as workers and servants.

I have also read where some earth historians who have written about this in the context of my people purposely setting out to create a slave race to satisfy our personal needs to work in the mines.

This hurts me that some think of us in this way, at least for those who actually believe we existed.”

“Geez Enki, I didn’t know you had feelings like that.”

"Well, perhaps you are seeing the soft side of a god but maybe I should have obliterated all of you to release myself of guilt."

"Yes, of course that would have made you feel better, I'm sure," I replied wondering if he really meant it.

"Sure we used early humans to replace our own people in the mines but do you think that the Annunaki were paid generous wages for mining gold while the new human workers were paid nothing and treated poorly? This may come as a surprise to you but it is not in our psyche to oppress. There were the others that came later who were quite good at that.

As well, I would like to inform you my friend that we have never adhered to a monetary system when we were on earth or on Nibiru. Money, as you call it and your financial system with its banking component came into existence only a few hundred years ago in earth history whereas prior to that, there was mostly bartering that took place. Goods in exchange for goods. Some earth societies used metal coins to represent certain amounts of value, that was tangible and exchangeable for other commodities of like value, but in my world no such system existed."

"This is interesting Enki," I said. "All I have ever known is the money system that is in place now and how it relates to everything we do. Do tell, how did you manage things on your home world without having to pay for it?"

"How curious," Enki began, "That a world would become so entrenched in such short order to a system that is unique and found nowhere else in the galaxy, a system that is enslaving in itself and you would have to ask me how we managed things.

First of all, the idea of ownership was not known to us. The planet Nibiru is a living entity as is your earth so who can own her. Who could be so arrogant as to say I own this little piece of the great mother. No one owned land as it was not theirs to own.

On Nibiru the things that one required for survival such as basic food and shelter was equally everyone's right to enjoy. So who could say I shall live here beside the lake in this nice place and eat wonderfully fresh and healthy foods while others live in a desert with little or nothing to eat? No one lived in magnificent mansions while others lived in squalid shacks or hovels. Everyone had equal access to the nutrients that were beneficial to their bodies as well as the shelter that protected them from the elements.

Those that performed necessary work were treated the same as those who performed the arts or those that trained and taught in the education centres."

"Aha," I exclaimed. "You were communists. I knew there was something funny about you."

Enki rolled his eyes and looked heavenward in a show of exasperation.

Seriously, I have read about your communist movement and it was a failure due mostly to the fact that those who tried to instigate the system were greedy bastards and lived in luxury while the general populace lived in abject poverty.

Remember what I said about religion and the brilliance of the concept to keep humans in a state of confusion. The same was true of the economic system called communism. Quite frankly, while we are on the subject of economic systems, your current system of so called capitalism is even more enslaving than religion or communism."

"How so Enki, how could capitalism be more enslaving than communism or enslaving at all?"

"You are a slave to the almighty dollar I have heard said. There is this prevailing attitude that the more money you have the better off you will be. This is not true, never was. It is a false concept.

I started to tell you about those that came to dominate and conquer your world after we left. I was saying that the use of religion became the tool of subservience that was used to keep the human population in check but it was the combination of religion and money that really caused your loss of freedom.

Our later analysis made us realize that it was not so much the invaders fault that earth and its people were so susceptible to manipulation. Those that came were from a negatively oriented society and they did what they do naturally. Dominate. Plus, the earth was an open zone since the veil was in place giving free access to all who wanted to participate.

The problem with earthlings was that you had no idea who you were, why you were here or where you had come from plus you were hopelessly gullible. You did not realize that all are one and emanate from the same source. You still do not realize that today. It's not entirely your fault since the veil is in place but there was the expectation that progress would occur to the point that you would see a glimmer of the Creator in yourselves."

"But you just finished telling me that the veil was supposed to hide all of that from us."

"Yes, that's true but through each successive life that you live you should see glimmers of the truth. Then after thousands of years and many hundreds of incarnations with all the information passed down to you, don't you think that you should start to get it by now?"

"Well maybe, I guess," I replied weakly.

Enki continued, "So when we left, humans looked skyward for the gods as the gods no longer lived amongst them. However, the new gods remained incognito and only appeared to special humans to give them special tasks. These humans were called prophets."

"You have been telling me this over and over, Enki, that the Old Testament was mostly about you and Enlil", I stated. "Other ancient texts also refer to Marduk and Ningishzidda as Thoth and Ra in Egypt and Quetzalcoatl and Veracocha in Mesoamerica.

It seems to make sense that there was, during ancient times, a family of gods that came from another place with advanced technologies that elicited the worship of man. It is even likely and certainly seems to fit the fossil record that there was a sudden advancement from Cro Magnon to Homo sapien which fits with your genetic tampering of our evolutionary progression.

The part I don't get however is why a thousand years later another series of sages, prophets and gods came back to further enlighten us. I am of course referring to Jesus, Mohammed and Buddha. Why did this new line of adepts come on the scene?" The original gods, the Annunaki, had left, so were these old recycled gods or were they actually new?"

"Both", replied Enki, "To use your terminology, Buddha and Jesus were recycled while Mohammed was new.

When we left Earth about the year 1500 BCE, by your reckoning, our intention was to never return as we had messed up your planet and did a huge disservice to your evolutionary progress. We should have left your planet and the indigenous people to develop along customary lines which even Enlil realized was the right thing to do. And this was really something for Enlil to admit that we had been wrong because quite frankly, he always thought that he was right.

But after time and with much reflection we realized that we had a commitment to make things right since we messed up in the first place. So with great thought and much debate we decided that we would send helpers.

The idea was that rather than try to reverse the damage that was done, we would simply try to educate mankind in the ways of the mind and spirit. So we sent Siddhartha Gautama whom you know as the Buddha.

His teachings were lofty and spiritual with the key being an attainment of nirvana through achievements on earth. The idea of reincarnation was introduced along with discipline, obedience and abstinence. The law of Karma also became apparent with his teachings.

We felt that this would give mankind a leg up, if you will, on matters pertaining to the soul and help overcome some of the left over vestiges of our ego fuelled adventures on Earth. Man needed to understand that he was much more than just flesh and blood. We knew this was true but kept it from you in the early days so we felt it was our duty to share these truths with you once we had gone.

Buddha was none other than Ninhursag, the great mother who helped me fashion Homo sapien from the cave-man in those early years on earth."

"I know this is a dumb question but at the risk of you calling me an idiot I am going to ask it anyways", I said. "Ninhursag was female in an Annunaki body and Siddhartha Gautama was clearly male. Can this occur under natural conditions?"

"Yes you are an idiot and that is a dumb question since you already know that even you have the ability to decide whether to be male or female," replied Enki. "It was generally agreed on Nibiru that a male would be most effective in delivering the message on earth and Ninhursag would be the most effective person to deliver it. The original gender of Ninhursag was not an issue.

Let me say however that the results were less than desired. We had overestimated your ability to grasp things that are spiritual in nature and quickly determined that our tact had been wrong. Even though Buddha delivered his message effectively and with loving care, the message did not have enough nutrients to bear fruit.

Thus, the teachings of the spirit were not understood at the time, but a foundation had been laid that we could use to continue our quest to enlighten humans. Or at the very least, try and keep you from killing each other.

Since all 3rd density beings are made up of mind/body/spirit the teachings of Buddha were only of the spirit and we realized afterwards that we needed a more comprehensive or balanced view. That being said, we sent a second emissary, one whose name you might recognize as Jesus Christ.

I have said many times, he was not the son of god. There is only The One Infinite Creator and we are all his sons but the funny part was that Jesus in fact was none other than Marduk, my son. Since I had posed as the great 'I Am' I guess that makes Jesus/Marduk my son."

"Ha ha Enki," I said. "That's a good joke."

"Yes, well", Enki continued. "Marduk had agreed to come back to earth and deliver the message of mind/body that would eventually supplement the spirit.

Now Marduk had some serious ego problems while he was on earth the first time around thinking that he was first among the Annunaki gods, but when we left and went back to Nibiru, our royal family debated at length on who should be send this time and it was Marduk's name that came up. He was ready and fit for the task.

Jesus/Marduk was to give a more balanced message which covered mind, body and soul. When Jesus/Marduk talked about his father in heaven he was literally referencing All That Is or The One Infinite Creator.

Your church fathers, wanting to build a powerful organization, distorted the words of Jesus/Marduk to suit their own needs. So much of what Jesus/Marduk said was misunderstood and again we found ourselves scratching our heads as to how we could possibly help you stubborn, inconceivably stupid race of people."

"Don't hold anything back," I said.

"Not all was lost," Enki went on as if he hadn't heard my little joke. "There were bits and pieces of information that went underground as the Roman Catholic Church came into prominence but for anyone seeking the truth, it was there, just not easy to find.

We also had to wait for your scientists to find our ancient cities and dig up the written records that we purposely left behind to enlighten the future generations of humans. We thought that they would be discovered sooner rather than later but when the dark ages came upon you, all sense of direction was lost."

Enki paused for several minutes as he seemed to be lost in thought. Then he spoke.

"You might find this hard to believe but we are a positively polarized society which may sound funny based on the way we acted in our early days on earth portraying ourselves as gods and demanding libations and sacrifice from the newly fashioned humans. But our intent was always honest and we are indeed brothers since we occupy the same solar system.

We did our best to right the wrong but it was easy for the message to be distorted and cause all sorts of confusion which has led to war and genocide on your planet over the centuries that followed.

The ancient writings all spoke of Armageddon which is the war to end all wars. I talked about this before as these things are signposts indicating a transition to 4th density and transformation to a new beginning. It will also be a very painful period that you must go through again as a test to push humans towards making up their minds on positive vs. negative polarity."

 "I get that Enki, about Armageddon and all," I replied. "But what about the promise of the return of the gods? In almost all the literature the gods promised one day to return. And yet here we are still waiting some 3000 years later for something to happen and you say maybe nothing will."

"Not quite what I said dear boy," Enki replied. "But I am glad you are listening and not asking stupid questions anymore. You see, both are happening and both have happened. It's your understanding of time that is messing you up. As I tried to explain before, time is circular and simultaneous and it's the illusion of time in your world that makes it seem linear.

The end of the world is happening as we speak and there is a transition in progress. Those ready for 4th density work will remain here while those destined to continue in 3rd density will be snatched away while thinking they are still here. See what I mean."

This wasn't even a moment for beer, I need tequila.

"Crystal clear Enki," I said as I rolled my eyes."

"As for the gods returning," Enki continued. "I am standing before you, living proof that the gods have returned. The glorious return of the gods turns out to be me and you chatting over a beer in the park. How about that for an ironic twist?"

The park was a public place and you weren't allowed any alcoholic beverages but Enki and I had snuck a couple beers under our jacket. It was quite ironic indeed.

"Many are destined to reinact 3rd density because they are too dumb to realize what's at stake. Few will proceed to 4th density where they will be transformed in body and mind to experience a million years in the study of the power of love. Mark my words, one or the other will happen to each and every individual who has ever set foot on this earth."

"OK, Enki, answer this," I replied. "There are 350 million people in the USA who every Sunday listen to preachers tell them how much god loves them and has forgiven their sins while promising everlasting bliss in heaven.

You, on the other hand have concocted a wild-ass story that most would see as fantasy or better yet, heresy. A hundred years ago you would have been burned at the stake. Funny thing is, your story makes more sense than Jesus saving me from eternal damnation as the son of a Jewish war-god who was a genocidal maniac.

You however are a mad-scientist from another planet that screwed-up our genetics, screwed-up our world and now have returned to tell us we are all screwed-up. Strangely enough, your explanations help me understand some of the crazy things that happen in our world. Your view of things also gives me a much better picture of what the afterlife looks like and takes the sting out of death.

So here's the question, how can we ever really know? There is not enough evidence nor enough proof one way or the other as to what is true and what isn't. I know the world is purposely made this way as you have told me countless times so what do you recommend?"

 "You know something," Enki replied. "For once you are exactly to the point and this is how I answer that.

Entities have been coming to this earth for thousands of years for the expressed purpose to gain experience and seek value fulfilment. Also throughout time, entities who agree to the mind/body/soul state have had a sub-ambition to slowly awaken to their real self while in the body. It doesn't do you a lot of good to realize this in your spirit form because you already know it.

In mind/body form you need to become aware of the spirit and the bigger picture. This is done slowly over many lives and if you are ready to awaken, then you are ready to move on.

If you are deeply involved in a world religion, it is not your time. If you pursue power and money, then it is not your time. If you kill, cheat, lie and steal, it is not time for you to transition.

If you seek to reason and understand why things happen the way they do, if you wonder who you are and what you are doing here, if you love to explore all the mysteries of life and seek balance in your life, then maybe you are ready. If you have a sense that there is something really important happening but can't quite put your finger on it, then you are ready.

Ultimately, you choose your polarity, knowingly or unknowingly. What matters is that you choose and that choice is reflected in your actions.

Then it is time. I don't give a hoot about all the folks who clearly aren't ready. They have many more lives to lead and another 75,000 year cycle before it becomes apparent to them that there is something more.

Besides, in a few hundred years, Christianity will have run its course and will be dead. It is already happening now with more and more young people opting for more rational explanations of the strange world they live in. Then more will be free to explore the mysteries just as they did in ancient Egypt three thousand years ago.

But you and a few others are on the cusp and that is why I am here. You are close to transitioning into 4th density if you play your cards right, as they say, otherwise you will be staying in 3rd for another 75,000 years.

This is perhaps the most difficult testing ground in the entire galaxy. The veil along with the intermixing of negative and positive polarities makes this plane of existence on earth challenging and demanding. The stakes are high and you need a gentle nudge to get you over the top and into fourth. It's like training for the marines; you have to push yourself to the limit."

"Enki, perhaps the real question is how will I know that my actions have reflected a choice for the positive or negative?"

This caused Enki to hesitate as he seemed to reflect for several seconds before saying...

"If you are aware of the polarities then you should know. It will be intuitive. If you are not aware then you are making a decision in the absence of knowing and it really doesn't matter. All will be known when you transition into spirit."

Chapter 16: The Transition

It has always been a favourite practice of mine to ask questions I already know the answers to. Sometimes it backfires but today I thought to try this on Enki while we were taking a stroll down one of the walking lanes in the downtown area of the city.

I had read much about how we transition from body to spirit or what was normally termed, death. Even in Tarot, the 'Death' card was meant to signify transition and so the idea was fairly well established but hugely misunderstood.

Dr. Michael Newton had written several books on this subject where he used hypnotic regression to take a person back through the birth experience into previous lives. The journey for me began after I realized that religious thought did not cover this subject very well. Christianity avoided this topic which was really too bad since even Jesus performed the death/resurrection ritual on Lazarus which I think might have been speaking to this point. Newton's book gave me the first hint of a new paradigm.

"Enki," I began. "Tell me about the death experience."

Enki looked at me and then held his head up just slightly, like a wolf testing the air for the scent of a nearby animal. He gazed around and then seemingly forgot that I had addressed him with a question. It was very peculiar behaviour, even for a god.

"Enki??"

He looked at me and then abruptly turned and walked away.

"Hey wait a darn minute," I said. "I don't think that was a dumb question, was it?"

Enki looked back at me and said, "I have another issue to take care of that has just come up. Sorry, but I'll have to talk to you later. Goodbye."

It was the way he said goodbye that had me perplexed. It was almost as if he was saying goodbye for good but I knew we had further things to discuss and I knew our work wasn't done. So why the heck was he acting so strange?

I was deep in thought and hadn't even realized that I had drifted off the walking path and onto the road. It was a road that only allowed service vehicles to operate but as I looked up my vision was filled with white, lots of white. In an instant I knew the white was that of a panel truck making a delivery in the area and that I had drifted off the walking path on a blind corner and the driver didn't see me. Suddenly a searing pain shot up and down my frame like two squirrels running in opposite directions along a tree.

That was it. A flash of white, a burst of pain, then blackness. The blackness lasted no longer than a second, certainly no longer than the time it took for the pain that I thought was going to be excruciating to suddenly vanish. It was all very strange.

It's not that I thought it was a bad dream or I was going to suddenly wake-up but there was a feeling of lightness or perhaps crispness and clarity. My dreams had always been a bit vague with a sense that there was nothing beyond the periphery of my vision other than shadowy, inconsistent scenes. My anticipation was that something was going to morph into something else or that nothing was really real. Dreams for me were always fuzzy around the edges like the early morning fog over a canola field in the late fall. This was not like that.

There was no fog or fuzziness. Everything was bright, clear and glimmering just like a summer day with the sun light reflecting off a lake creating a dazzling light show. Sounds were crisp and clear like little girls screaming at the water park. I hated those shrill screams.

The feeling that I was floating was not particularly alarming to me as this was quite common in my dreams but what got my attention was the scene below me. It was me, lying on the pavement below with blood oozing from both ears and my chest squashed flat.

Since there were tire marks on my chest and blood pooling around my head it didn't take much to deduce what had happened. It actually came as no surprise that I was dead. The body that I had inhabited for 60 years was dead and gone. I had bought the farm sort of speak. Pining for the fiords as they say.

It was like all that stuff I had read and all that stuff that Enki had talked about was brought to reality in an instant. The new reality of me in my true energetic form was what I was currently experiencing.

I was seeing everything below me in brilliant clarity, I mean everything. Like when the Terminator is driving down the middle of the road in the pitch black with no headlights and young John Connor asks, "Can you see anything?" and Arnold answers, "I see everything."

I remembered when Enki did something weird to me and caused me to see energy patterns instead of solid objects. Now I was seeing energy patterns as well as solid objects. It wasn't one or the other as with Enki that day; it was both at the same time. I could see the energy wave slowing in frequency and freezing into solid shapes like water in an ice cube tray. It was more like I could read the energy signature and determine what it was suppose to be before it actually became what it was going to be.

The energy signature of concrete differed from wood and an ant was different from a pebble due to its pulse or frequency. Not because I could see the color and grain in a piece of wood or the shape and rigidity of concrete but because the atoms gave off a color and pulsed like the bars on a graphic equalizer when Stairway to Heaven is playing. I kind of felt special.

People were collecting below and I could see they were human in shape with blobs of shimmering protoplasm around them. Some were yelling for help while others were screaming and trying to look away but the awful draw of a dead body was too much. I could feel the energy of the thoughts of those below. The sounds of the voices were coming to me as colours rather than noise but I could hear their words as well.

As I was trying to absorb the radical nature of my new reality I had this overwhelming urge to keep everyone away from my recently discarded hunk of flesh only to realize that the task was impossible in my current state plus I was holding on to something that was no longer needed.

The ambulance eventually came and my cold lifeless body was lifted onto a stretcher and loaded into the back. I wondered if I would feel anything as they strapped me down but no such luck. The attachment to my body had faded quickly and was now gone. I did however detect the faint energy signature of the bacteria that had already begun the process of decomposition. In a few days, that energy display would be dominant.

It struck me as funny that the shock of my untimely death had worn off so quickly and that my new energetic state was so comfortable, so natural and normal. In my previous body I had had five senses with which to experience the world around me but now in my new energy state, it seemed that I had at least fifteen more at my fingertips even though I didn't have fingertips anymore. I couldn't describe what the senses were but I knew I had them as I became more indoctrinated in my new world. A world that seemed immense and layered.

I watched the scene below unfold and noticed other beings appearing at about the same height above ground as I was. These were non-human entities that were looking for the newly departed spirit, me.

I didn't feel threatened or like I needed to run and hide somewhere even though these beings were dark and foreboding. They definitely shied away from the light that surrounded us so I assumed they were the dark force entities that Enki had talked about and so I approached and sent out the thought projection, 'how's it going guys'.

As I got near, although near was not an accurate description since space was different in my current state, the entities grasped my presence and unravelled my thought projection at the same time. It was one of my newfound senses that made me realize that compared to my new dark force friends, I was a glowing ball of light. As soon as they saw me, they disappeared in a puff. Gone, like a small ice cube in a warm gin and tonic.

That got me thinking if a guy could get a nice cold beer up here somewhere and maybe catch a ballgame while those below organized themselves to take my body away. Then a funny thing happened. In a flash, I was sitting in a lounge with huge plate glass windows looking out onto the ball field in the middle of the third inning during a Jays and Cubs game.

I was sure enough at a table and the beer that sat in front of me looked real. There was frost on the outside of the mug with little bubbles rising to the surface on the inside making a lovely foam head. I reached for it expecting the mug to disappear or my hand to pass through it, since after all, I was dead and I really did not expect to drink a beer at a ball game in my current state.

Humouring myself, I reached for the glass and it felt like a mug full of beer, nice and cold, then I took a sip. It was glorious, cool and crisp with a tangy after taste. At that point I realized that the experience of drinking a beer, the whole sensation of it was from memory. Memory so precise, so exact that drinking a beer in my formerly alive body was only experienced through the sense of taste and feel. In that body it was a series of nerve endings firing and sending signals to my brain that a beverage was draining down my throat.

Now, the sensation was more direct, more vivid, more enchanting. There were no nerve endings or synapses to get in the way of experiencing a cool crisp barley sandwich finding its way down my throat to dance and tingle its way through my new energy circuits. The taste and feel was glorious.

I was learning things about my new abilities at a torrid pace when I realized that my body was headed for the morgue while I was at a ball game having a beer and lollygagging. I should probably be at the morgue to make sure everything was being handled properly.

Then I saw my body strapped to a flat white slab and I was floating above it. I was at the ball game too. My beer was half gone and the

Jays scored a run forcing me to my feet cheering with everyone else but of course no one could see or hear me. Meanwhile, at the same time, I was watching some doctor cut me open to see which part of me had got squished.

It was slowly becoming evident that I could be in several places at the same time as space had taken on a new meaning as Enki had tried to explain. Time was different too as I was in the ever present now. Whew, this would take some getting used to as there was neither day nor night, seasons or otherwise, except the memory of such. There was just the present moment with a diffuse light all around.

Then I wondered about where my memory and thoughts were coming from.

My thoughts, I thought, were coming from somewhere else since I had no grey matter or bone to house the brain where I had previously thought my thoughts came from.

But they seemed to generate from right inside my own energy grid. They were like electromagnetic pulses generating outward from my own conscious energy form as if they were a real living thing. I had always known that thoughts were important but I was never exposed to how real and effectual they were until now. Except maybe that time Enki had me walking around, like a dork, looking at energy patterns and seeing how my thoughts affected blobs.

This was only scratching the surface of the art of thought. I was also aware that thoughts acted as a transportation device whereby I could access any part of the galaxy merely by thinking where I wanted to go.

Enki had shown me how to travel using my dreaming body but now in my energetic state, travel was easier, more direct and instantaneous.

I also had this strange inkling that I could manipulate energy with controlled thought to create almost anything I wanted. As I became more entrenched in my new state there was a distant memory like a dream within a dream that I had created a world. The memory wasn't fully formed yet but I could see this world as if it was covered with clouds and in a state of early formation. I knew the memory would come to me in time.

As for memory, I was accessing it from some giant storage grid that was all around me and contained every bit of human experience recorded in bright living color. My access point was the recognition of a familiar energy pattern within the grid unique to mine. Just like inserting a key into the front door of your home. I was conscious energy with no form but every bit alive as I've ever been.

As for my surroundings, there was a constant diffuse light all around me which appeared to project into the 3rd density earth plane as energy beams illuminating objects that I was then able to observe on earth. The energy beams penetrated objects causing them to glow like those parties back in the 70's when everyone's tee shirt glowed because of a black light some guy had in his basement.

The diffuse light also seemed to energize my field and cause a renewed vigour. If I didn't know better, I was being refuelled by the light. It was like getting up on a bright clear sunny morning full of energy after a good night's sleep and going for a run along a hard packed sandy beach.

I never got tired and there was no evidence of the day's end in my new world so as far as I could tell, it was a continual bright clear sunny morning. I had the sense that a million years could go by and it would seem like a day. Hmmmm, wasn't sure if that was a good thing especially if one got bored easily. That could make for some awful long hours of staring at the ceiling or reading crummy novels.

I was contemplating a host of weird thoughts when out of the diffuse light I could see a shiny object approaching me. At one point I thought it might be an alien vessel coming to check me out but as it got closer, I could see the energy imprint. It was somebody not something and as it approached the energy signature changed and suddenly I was standing in front of Pope John XXIII. He was holding a staff and in full robes with the little white beanie cap on the back of his head. I could see the thought projection emanating towards me saying, "Thou hast sinned and for thy transgressions thou shalt be cast into the depths of hell for a couple million years or so, and see how you like it."

"Holy shit," I thought. "All that stuff Enki was feeding me was crap. Damn, I'm in the same boat as Josef Stalin, Pol Pot and Andy Griffith. Damn. I don't even know where the Andy Griffiths thought came from. Damn, I'm in a tight spot."

Then my head, or maybe my energetic head exploded with a really loud thought coming from the new energy presence. It went something like hahahahahaha, you gullible son of a bitch.

The energy blob that had been the pope started to morph, change shape and change into something familiar.

I took an intense gaze or should I say scan and the next thing I knew I was looking at my best friend from 3 lives ago. Amazingly, an instant later I was looking at my father, then brother, then son, then wife. There were so many relationships I had with this entity over the many lives I had led that it looked like a movie played on fast forward right before my eyes. Holy shit I thought, maybe all those personalities were emanating from the same soul source.

"Of course they are you damn fool," the thought came back. "Look past what you think you 'see' and look for the energy signature."

So I did and then it became glaringly apparent that the entity before me was for all and intense purposes my closest friend/wife/brother/son over that past million years.

"How is this possible," I thought. "Why are you here now?"

"Finally, you have your wits about you. Took you long enough to recognize me and recover from the death experience. Thought you would get through it quicker than that but you were always a little thick."

As he/she projected that thought, everything about him/her became familiar again. We have been together for so many lives and had been very close, always.

"So what are you doing?" I thought.

"Just what I am supposed to do," came the reply. "Take you home, as you have done for me a thousand times previous, but not before having played a pretty good joke on you."

"Yes, that was a good one, the pope drifting out of mid air to condemn me to everlasting hell."

"Yeah, well you were pretty hung up on religion for far too many lives and this was the one life that broke you of the habit so I threw that in to remind you what a dumb shit you've been for the last thousand years."

"Thanks for that," I said as the memories started to flood in like a mountain creek during spring run-off.

All the things we had done together were at my finger tips. It took no time at all to go back over a thousand lives we had spent together under all sorts of different conditions, circumstances and relationships.

"Are you ready to go home now or do you need more time?"

"I think I need more time. I want to say goodbye to all the people I have been close to this past life and more importantly, I want to be at my funeral."

"Fine, just let me know when you are ready and I'll come and get you and take you to the light, even though I suspect you could find your way quite easily now."

"You're right, I have a sense of where I need to go but since you are my guide, I wouldn't want to mess with your duties so I will give the thumbs up when I am ready."

"Cool, dude, see you in a thousand years or a couple of seconds, whichever comes first."

And with that my closest ally for multiple millennia was gone.

Chapter 17: Party On

It seemed like only a few seconds had passed before I wanted to be at my funeral. A mere thought and a little jig took me where I needed to be. I was really getting used to sliding back and forth in time and space.

There it was, a nice big gathering place, just like I had pictured, no church as I had told my kids and wife, but a simple gathering in an architecturally sound structure. The proceedings had started so I drifted into a little corner up near the ceiling where I could see everything.

I laughed as my positioning was not needed since I saw everything from everywhere. What I would have given to have had this ability when I went to The Who concert back in the 70's.

I watched as person after person got up and said nice things about me, some true and some not so true but it didn't matter. I was flattered and that was important. It's funny how people say mostly nice things about the dead. It's as if you'll get haunted if you say something nasty.

I had made a difference in many peoples' lives however and I had the respect of my peers, children and wife. Somehow it all seemed just right and after the speeches were over, everyone proceeded to get drunk. Just like I had wanted.

A feeling of extreme warmth and satisfaction came over me and suddenly I was amongst everyone dancing and shaking hands but of course no one felt my hand but maybe more than one person had the feeling that I was near.

I was bopping and weaving to the sound of 54-40 when I inadvertently put both thumbs in an upwards motion, at least energetically I performed the motion and within seconds a bright flash appeared and my friend of countless millennia was there with a big grin imprinted on his blob of glowing embers.

I wasn't sure I was ready to go but then what else was there to do? The party would go on for a few more hours but I had a million years to replay how much fun I had had. Not just at the party but my entire life.

Now that I had all of my lives in rich and brilliant color right in front of me as if I was reliving them, it was at that instant it occurred to me that my last life was the best of the best.

I had done all the things that were important to me. It was a perfect way to transition.

OK, I said. Let's go.

My friend gently guided me towards the golden white light that I knew was expecting me.

As we drifted upwards I could see all the spiritual realms layered above and below.

I could see inside the earth where the lack of light seemed most acute. That was where the dark force entities lived. They were rising to the earth's surface and going about their nasty business then escaping back down to the darkness when they were done. I could see clearly that these entities had no real power but just the same, they were able to cause havoc and pain. They seemed to be able to penetrate the blob form of humans and influence their behaviour, usually negatively.

Then there was the area on or near the surface of the earth that was not as black as where the dark force entities lived but was varying shades of grey that appeared like dark and swirling storm clouds. I could see this was where all sorts of entities were thrashing about, crashing into each other and generally existing in a state of mayhem. These entities were not penetrating the human blobs like the dark force entities but were influencing behaviours by various other physical means.

I could see clearly what Enki had been talking about when he said that there were others that came when the Annunaki left. They stayed incognito and hidden but their influence in the world was real. I could see them.

As I continued to rise the light became more intense and I could see that those below, although there were no restrictions, were confined to the lower realms mostly because they were unable to withstand the light. It was like being caught on a bright clear winter day with the sun reflecting off the snow and having forgotten your sunglasses. It's really quite painful to those who are not accustomed to the light.

I could sense their pain as they tried to follow me up but were deflected back down by the intensity of the light. It was like a force-field preventing the ascent of these lower beings as they could not stand the penetration of the light.

Perhaps they would require a few thousand more incarnations on Earth to figure out how the transition to light works.

I guess I had figured it out since I continued to rise and was not restricted by the intensity of the light like the others. I wondered how it was happening and why the ever-increasing intensity of light did not seem to bother me. It was as if I somehow absorbed the photons into my energetic shell. I could see that there was still much for me to learn.

Then, just like that, I felt as if I had reached, or should I say, come home to a place where everything felt familiar. From all around, seemingly out of nowhere, I was swarmed by energetic entities swirling around me like a bunch of teenage boys wanting to get close to the prom queen. As I sensed the energy of the entities around me, I was filled with a great joy. These were all my best friends, closest acquaintances, intimate lovers and practically everything in-between.

In a kaleidoscope of memories, emotion and feelings I was experiencing my relationship with hundreds of these close friends in a simultaneous fashion all over again. Everything that was special to me was being relived in absolute vivid clarity.

I am not sure if it took thirty seconds, thirty years or thirty thousand years to review all the memories but it didn't matter as time didn't factor in and I was just enjoying the sheer bliss of it all.

What surprised me, however, was the entities I knew that were still living on Earth and still incarnate were also with me here. I was confused at first and it showed because I was immediately presented with a thought.

"Remember, you can be in two places at the same time. In fact you can be in ten worlds, five time zones and three lives at the same time if you want. Of course you can be here as well since this is home for all of us."

"Well I guess that makes perfect sense," I thought. It was really quite overwhelming and it would take some time to absorb all the new stuff but in the meantime I was having a blast.

The party would have lasted for at least another century I'm sure had I not got the distinct notion that I was being summoned. The notion only lasted a moment as moments go but then I was presented with a powerful thought projection saying something like we require your presence.

It wasn't that we require your presence at a specific location, like meet us on Saturn at 5PM. It was get your ass to where we are now. Where they were or who they were I didn't have a clue but as things work in the afterlife my next thought was that I had better get there, where ever it was that 'there' meant.

True to form, in an instant I was standing in a great hall with huge pillars holding up a giant ornate ceiling structure complete with sacred geometric carvings of all sorts. I had never seriously studied sacred geometry during any of my lives on earth so I could not discern the meaning or intent other than to just recognize the form and be appreciative of it.

Then it occurred to me that I was actually seeing a structure just like back on earth. Not energetic representations or memory manifestations but real stone pillars and marble floors. I could feel the warm marble on my feet. Wait a minute, I have feet?

Somehow in the time it took for me to get from my gala home coming to this palace, I was standing in a solid body in a solid place. It kind of reminded me of the holodeck on the Enterprise. Very real.

Then the solid form of the giant amphitheatre morphed into an even more giant throne room with twelve golden thrones surrounding me. Damn, I thought, if Yahweh comes through that door over there I'm buggered. It will be hell for a couple of eternities I thought, no pleading for mercy here.

Then a wavy energy field moved across each of the 12 thrones like a mirage that one sees in the desert which makes one think there is water nearby and just like that I was standing in the middle of the twelve ascended masters. Or so I thought.

"I knew this was important shit so I had better be on my best behaviour, no jokes," I thought. I wished Enki was here as I had a sense that he would be a good guy to have around right about now. I even thought that thinking of Enki might bring him in but no such luck.

I put on my most serious face although I wasn't sure which of the several hundred faces I had during all my lives would serve as serious but whichever one it was I made it as serious as I could.

Then the giant being directly in front of me stood up and announced," I am the great I Am" and trumpets sounded.

My knees went weak as I started to feel them buckle. My head was spinning and I thought I was going to faint, like I had lost a bet, a really really big bet. I had bet all of eternity that Jehovah didn't exist and yet here I was in the process of being judged. I was starting to imagine the heat from the fires of hell licking at my balls.

Maybe if I tell them I was just kidding about all that stuff that I said back on earth I might get off easy. Damn, I was in a tight spot.

Then a huge roar of laughter broke out from all around me and the giant god-like beings morphed into Gandalf-like figures with long beards and staffs, only not so old and haggard looking as what the real Gandalf looked like. More like what Gandalf might have looked like when he was a teenager.

I'm sure the look on my face was reason enough for the laughter because I must have looked somewhat dumbfounded.

"We got you didn't we.....hahahahaha. Thought I was the lord god Jehovah didn't ya, hahaha. Serves you right since we could see there was still that little bit of doubt left in your energy imprint. We literally had to scare the bejesus out of you. Well, have you nothing to say? Come on lad, speak up."

"Ummm, well, ummmm," was the only thing I could muster.

"That's brilliant, ummmmm."

"Well, you see sir, I started to say as I looked at the ground."

At that point, I realized that the ascended masters had a sense of humour. That and the uproarious laughter that erupted all around me. I looked up and everyone was smiling at me which was good considering these were pretty advanced beings, I suppose.

"Now listen," was the thought that was projected into my head. We are here to tell you that you have graduated to 4th density by way of your polarity. Good job ol' boy."

It seemed like I was at a British country club but maybe Enki was right about all that density stuff. Maybe everything that Enki said was right.

"Of course he was right," was the projection that came forcefully back into my head. "Did you think he was pulling your bloody leg??"

I still hadn't really gotten used to the idea that everyone and their dog could listen in on my thoughts so I had to be careful because I still had stupid shit running around inside my head.

"Wow, fourth density. When do I start, how do I prepare, what's next?"

I was really excited by the news plus I was trying to hide the fact that I was looking and acting like an idiot in front of the masters of the universe. No one wants to look like a tool in front of company such as that.

"You don't need to prepare, you can start now or in a million years whichever you prefer. You don't have to go to 4th either if that is your desire. You can go back to 3rd again if you want. You've done it before. But if you do decide to go into 4th we highly recommend you stay here for a while and get fully re-energized before your next excursion.

 "Wait a minute I thought, sort of out loud. What do you mean that I have gone back to 3rd before, which presupposes, I suppose, that I have been in 4th before?"

"You actually achieved 5th density many earth revolutions ago. Then you made the rare choice to go back to 3rd as you possessed the not so common desire to go backwards rather than forwards."

"Whoa partner," was the thought that came out quicker than I could think to stop it, which I dearly hoped was not too John Wayneish or flippant. "I was in 5th and then went back to 3rd? I didn't even know what to ask next. Would this be considered stupid in your circles?"

"Well, kind of. More laughter. No, actually we get a few folk wanting to go backwards instead of forward for many different reasons but we always support the entity in its desires whatever direction they choose to move."

"OK, so I went from third to fourth to fifth then back to third now I'm ready for fourth for a second time. Am I making any sense to anyone?"

"Sure you are. The memories of who you are have not fully come back to you yet. You will realize the journey that you have chosen and the meaning of it in good time. In the meantime we think that you did not spend the requisite amount of time in 4th density on your last trip through so our recommendation is that you spend more time in fourth. You short-circuited fourth last time due to your accelerated evolution. More time in this density will be highly beneficial to you, is our belief, but as always it is your choice."

"Thank you for sharing this information with me and as all my memories come back I will take your kind suggestion to heart and consider all my options. Do I still have access to the viewing room?"

"Yes, indeed you do but with 4th density earth experience the viewing room becomes less important. This is because your life span is greatly expanded compared to life on earth in 3rd density. Viewing the major incidents and choosing your companions and parents ahead of time simply does not matter anymore. The veil is lifted and your entire reason for being changes in fourth and as does the work that you will do."

"But doesn't it matter that I choose my parents in 4th like i did in 3rd?"

"Those around you are all positively oriented and so you could be born to a pair of hyenas and it really wouldn't matter much."

"Ok, so even if it doesn't matter can I still drop by the viewing room and check out what's up."

"Sure, no problem, but we have to go now as we have other stuff to attend."

"Right, it's been fun, take care", and with that the twelve grand masters again became a wavy mirage of energy apparitions spinning away like pinwheels at a good fireworks display. Since these guys have a magnificent sense of humour I imagined them giggling and laughing as they sizzled and spun away.

Then, just as quick, another batch of memories came cascading back into my energy field. Upon reflection of these past and present experiences I became aware that I was still incarnated in seven different bodies on four different planets. Holy cow, I thought, I've been busy and it now made sense what the one who called himself "I Am" was trying to say.

From this knowledge I could take inventory of the energy levels in my gestalt and sure as shit I was down a quart. From memories of previous experience in 4th density a good 80 – 95% of my total current energy level was needed for the work ahead but current inventory suggested that I was at 50% presently. I felt like a Prius, god forbid.

I was not quite sure what I needed to do other than the obvious, which was wait for my other selves to kick the bucket and join back into the gestalt. It was kind of fun thinking how many personalities had been melded into what I was calling me.

On earth, I would have been diagnosed as a sick, deranged, multiple-personality, psycho son of a bitch. Here, however, it almost seemed like I was one of the advanced ones. Seems like all that crazy shit in my head was just normal after all.

I found my way to the viewing room just by thinking viewing room and poof I was there. I was really getting used to the whole 'space has no meaning' thing and not having to get in my truck and drive for two hours to get somewhere while listening to Jackson Browne tell me how much he likes singing songs or Steve Earle about how much he likes growing dope along Copper Head Road or John Denver going on about some country road. Hey wait a minute John is up here somewhere and I'm gonna have to look him up.

The viewing room was made to seem like a physical place for the convenience of blokes like me that were fresh out of body. I picked a chair and the screens appeared in a 3-dimensional array all around me. I could see all the screens simultaneously which was way cool. It was kind of like in the Exorcist where Linda Blair could move her head all the way around.

I was going to use the viewing room to glance into the 4th density life that was ahead of me but instead I got distracted and started looking at an early 3rd density world that was in a different galaxy. I was trying to make the connection as why that world seemed so familiar and why it was being shown to me. Then it occurred to me that this was the very world that Enki and I had visited and I made a startling realization.

People were going about their normal lives with this amazingly beautiful landscape spread out across the entire world. Everything was familiar because I had been a significant co-creator in this world. I had been involved in the design and had built all of the mountains, lakes and trees along with the whole eco-system that went with it. One area was especially important to me as I had taken special care to organize the photons that were the basic building blocks to construct an especially beautiful mountain range.

I had even designed a few animal species that lived in this mountainous area which I had specifically made to adapt to the particular terrain. I had held the whole design in my mind and then patiently pieced it all together.

Of course I had many friends who were there to help with other aspects of the geographical area. It occurred to me that other beings similar to me had created all the neat and cool places on earth too. I had even used some of these ideas, like the areas I enjoyed hiking in the Canadian Rockies to help create my own little part of this new world.

Enki knew when we were there that I was tied into the creation grid of the planet and even when I remarked at how beautiful certain aspects of the geography were, he just smiled and never said a thing. That rat.

Upon further reflection, I also realized that I had done most of my creative work on the newly formed world while asleep in my last life as a human on earth. Some mornings I would get up feeling exhausted. I guess anyone would after creating a mountain or two. Don't make mountains out of mole-hills took on a fresh new meaning.

I had made a lot of realizations in short order however I wasn't fooling myself. It might have been ten thousand years of equivalent time.

Then the screen turned to earth right around the time I had departed. I could see my other 2 selves in stark contrast to one another. In one life, I was a female in Europe with a family and small circle of close friends while in the other I was a small boy in a remote village somewhere along the Amazon River in Brazil.

Wow, quite divergent I thought. I wondered why I had chosen those two lives when the screen changed in conjunction with a new flood of memories. I was presented with the reasons. Since these lives were a further depiction of who I was, it was a further refining of the real me that I was trying to create and evolve into.

Revelations went on like this for hours which could have been years and I was totally amazed but not surprised at how enjoyable an experience it was.

Then just like that, three selves had checked back in and merged into the gestalt and the memory stick grew threefold while the batteries were recharged. I revelled as we reviewed the lives I had had on other planets in other solar systems in the galaxy we call the Milky Way.

I knew the other four were close to finishing up as well so I thought it would be a good time to visit all my buddies, friends and family that had been incarnating with me for the past 75,000 years on earth.

I organized the party by creating a big frat house with kegs of beer in every room, old couches, really ugly drapes, stains in the rug and holes in the gyproc from guys throwing beer bottles. I sent out the thought projected invitation and implored everyone to clothe themselves in their most recognizable bodies from which-ever era they chose to represent.

Everyone arrived, almost instantaneously, then all 357 of us sat around for two million years and drank beer and told stories about all the lives we had lived, all the stupid things we had done and of course all the most memorable moments.

Each time a collective memory was brought up it was re-enacted as if we were all floating in the sky above the scene where the event took place. We laughed and joked at each other as event after event paraded past us. Each of my friends and family had multiple choices of multiple events to relive and it was the best party I had ever been to.

Finally I got up and jumped on the couch and said, "Quieten down everyone. I have a few words to say."

"Hey sit down, the beers aren't finished yet," yelled my friend who had acted as my spirit guide in my last life.

"Look", I said. "If I have to come over there and shut your ugly mouth, I will."

Everyone laughed, but eventually all was quiet and I started to speak.

"It's been a hell o'va run boys and girls and as everyone knows I am off to the fourth for my next phase of work. But let me say this, I will never forget you guys as you have been the best bunch of ghosts I have ever had the pleasure of working with. You all will work through your karma in third and when the next harvest comes along I expect to see all of you in fourth and I will save a place at the table for you."

"Hey," chimed in my mother/brother/sister/aunt from 15 different lives. "What makes you think that you are off to 4th density by yourself?"

I must have looked like a deer in the headlights.

"Well, I've been harvested and I really didn't think any of you had since I would have probably known. Don't you think?"

Everyone erupted into laughter. It seemed like I was the brunt of everybody's jokes these days and that all my so-called friends and family had purposely blocked their thought projections so I had no idea everyone had graduated to the fourth. Since I was the last one to check in I guess it seemed like a good joke to everyone.

"Dammit all anyways you guys," I projected to the group. "Does everyone have to be a comedian? Doesn't anybody take anything serious up here?"

"Here, here ol' boy," my good friend in the back said. "Let's all raise our glasses to the man of the hour or should I say millennia."

There was a gigantic clink of glasses

"Thanks eh." I said keeping with good Canadian grammar.

I knew however it was time to make my way to the hub where the directional tunnels exist that guide us into the next incarnation. Seems like I was the last one to graduate from 3rd but the first to reincarnate to 4th density. Whoa.

I knew the masters would not meet me this time along the way, as they usually did when going into 3rd density, with words of encouragement. Going into fourth was kind of like going to University where you don't need your mom to hold your hand like in Grade 1.

As my memories continued to update I realized that the Grand Masters of the Universe were really good guys and I had spent a lot of time with them. They had caught me off guard the other day, or whenever that was, and scared the hell out of me, quite literally.

As I headed towards the 4th density tunnel, there is no veil there so a lot of things that an entity has to do to get ready for 3rd just weren't necessary for fourth.

But alas it was time. I had reached the hub and my fourth density entrance was ready for me as were the circumstances on earth. My pregnant mother was just going into labour so I really had to get a move on and thank god she wasn't a hyena.

The incarnational process always reminded me of a water slide. A really high water slide where you sit at the top take a deep breath and then launch yourself onto the slippery downward trough. Just like the one at West Edmonton Mall water-park where you had to squeeze the cheeks of your ass tight at the bottom otherwise you would experience the wonderful sensation of a water enema.

There I was, at the top of my slippery tunnel waiting for the green light, figuratively speaking of course.

"Holy shit," I thought. "Here I am ready to take the plunge again. Look out fourth density, here I come."

 I took a deep breath and then launched myself into the maelstrom of dazzling lights and spinning fields of sizzling energy, maybe just like being right inside the fireworks this time.

"Geronnnamooooooo"